Garrett Surname

Ireland: 1600s to 1900s

From Ireland Church Records of Baptism, Marriage and Death

Comprised of Roman Catholic and Church of Ireland Records

From Counties Carlow, Cork, Kerry and Dublin City

Compiled by **Donovan Hurst**

February 1, 2013

Dedication

This work is dedicated to all of those that came before us and shaped our lives to make us the people that we are today.

Table of Contents

Introduction

This is a compilation of individuals who have the surname of Garrett that lived in the country of Ireland from the 1600s to the 1900s. I have placed each entry into one of four categories: Families, Individual Births/Baptisms, Individual Burials, and Individual Marriages. If a marriage entry primarily concerns an Individual Garrett whom is female, then I have placed that entry under the category of Individual Marriages. If a marriage entry primarily concerns an Individual Garrett whom is male, then I have placed that entry under the category of Families. Images of many of these listings are available at http://churchrecords.irishgenealogy.ie/churchrecords/.

To help guide the reader of this work, the format of this book is as follows:

- Main Family Entry (Husband and Wife) (Father and Mother)

  o Child of Main Family Entry, including Spouse(s) when available

    ▪ Grandchild of Main Family Entry, including Spouse(s) when available

      • Great-Grandchild of Main Family Entry, including Spouse(s) when available

(**Bolded Text**) following any entry includes any additional information such as Residence(s), Occupation(s), Signature(s), etc. when available.

Hurst

Some of the fonts used in this work symbolizes Celtic writing. The traditional letters, numbers, and punctuation marks and their Celtic counterparts are as follows:

Traditional Letters (Uppercase & Lowercase)

A a B b C c D d E f G g H h I i J j K k L l M m N n O o P p Q q R r S s T t U u V v W w X x Y y Z z

Celtic Letters (Uppercase & Lowercase)

A a B b C c D ð E e F ꝼ G g H h I i J j K k L l M m

N n O o P p Q q R ʀ S s T t U u V ʋ W w X x Y ʒ Z z

Traditional Numbers

1 2 3 4 5 6 7 8 9 10

Celtic Numbers

1 2 3 4 5 6 7 8 9 10

Traditional Punctuation

. , : ' " & - ( )

Celtic Punctuation

. , : ' " & - ( )

Garrett Surname Ireland: 1600s to 1900s

Parish Churches

Carlow (Church of Ireland)

Aghold Parish, Carlow Parish, Dunleckney Parish, Painestown Parish, and Urglin Parish.

Cork & Ross (Roman Catholic or RC)

Aughadown Parish, Bandon Parish, Bantry Parish, Caharagh Parish, Clonakilty Parish, Clontead Parish, Cork - South Parish, Cork - SS. Peter & Paul Parish, Courcy's Country or Ballinspittal Parish, Kinsale Parish, Rossalettiri & Kilkeraunmor (Roscarbery & Lissevard) Parish, and Tracton Abbey Parish.

Dublin (Church of Ireland)

Arbour Hill Barracks Parish, Clontarf Parish, Glasnevin Parish, Kilmainham Parish, Leeson Park Parish, North Strand Parish, Rathmines Parish, Rotunda Chapel Parish, Sandford Parish, St. Anne Parish, St. Audoen Parish, St. Barnabas Parish, St. Bride Parish, St. Catherine Parish, St. George Parish, St. James Parish, St. John Parish, St. Jude Parish, St. Luke Parish, St. Mark Parish, St. Mary Parish, St. Michael Parish, St. Michan Parish, St. Nicholas Within Parish, St. Nicholas Without

Parish, St. Paul Parish, St. Peter Parish, St. Stephen Parish, St. Thomas Parish, and St. Werburgh Parish.

Dublin (Roman Catholic or RC)

Chapelizod Parish, Harrington Street Parish, Rathmines Parish, SS. Michael & John Parish, St. Agatha Parish, St. Andrew Parish, St. Audoen Parish, St. Catherine Parish, St. James Parish, St. Lawrence Parish, St. Mary Parish, St. Mary, Haddington Road, St. Mary, Pro Cathedral Parish, St. Michan Parish, and St. Nicholas Parish.

Kerry (Church of Ireland)

Kilnaughtin Parish.

Kerry (Roman Catholic or RC)

Killarney Parish.

Families

- Abraham Garrett, b. 1779, bur. 31 Jul 1841 (Burial, **St. Paul Parish**) & Mary Garrett

  - Arthur Garrett – bapt. 30 Apr 1823 (Baptism, **St. Paul Parish**), bur. 1 Apr 1825 (Burial, **St. Paul Parish**)

  - Jane Garrett – bapt. 6 Feb 1825 (Baptism, **St. Paul Parish**)

Abraham Garrett (father):

Residence - Mary's Lane - before July 31, 1841

Age at Death - 62 years

- Andrew Garrett & Jane Unknown

  - Margaret Garrett & John Roach – 28 Oct 1874 (Marriage, **St. Andrew Parish (RC)**)

    - Patrick James Roach – b. 1879, bapt. 1879 (Baptism, **St. Andrew Parish (RC)**)

    - Ellen Mary Roach – b. 1880, bapt. 1880 (Baptism, **St. Andrew Parish (RC)**)

    - John Joseph Roach – b. 1883, bapt. 1883 (Baptism, **St. Andrew Parish (RC)**)

    - Andrew William Roach – b. 27 Jan 1885, bapt. 6 Feb 1885 (Baptism, **St. Mary, Pro Cathedral Parish (RC)**)

    - Tomasina Mary Roach – b. 27 Mar 1888, bapt. 2 Apr 1888 (Baptism, **St. Mary, Pro Cathedral Parish (RC)**)

Hurst

Margaret Garrett (daughter):

Residence - 2 Upper Erne Street - October 28, 1874

John Roach, son of James Roach (son-in-law):

Residence - 118 Townsend Street - October 28, 1874

1879

1880

1883

39 Upper Gloster Street - February 6, 1885

59 Upper Gloster Street - April 2, 1888

Wedding Witnesses:

Michael O'Brien & Elizabeth Garrett

- o   Elizabeth Garrett & Thomas Lynch – 16 Dec 1875 (Marriage, **St. Andrew Parish (RC)**)
  - ▪ Mary A. Lynch – b. 7 May 1876, bapt. 14 May 1876 (Baptism, **Rathmines Parish (RC)**)

Elizabeth Garrett (daughter):

Residence - 136 Great Brunswick Street - December 16, 1875

Thomas Lynch, son of John Lynch & Anne Unknown (son-in-law):

Residence - 23 Brunswick Street - December 16, 1875

Richmond Street - May 14, 1876

Wedding Witnesses:

Peter Garrett & Jane Garrett

Garrett Surname Ireland: 1600s to 1900s

- Andrew Garrett & Unknown

  o Jane Garrett & Patrick Short – 1 Jun 1889 (Marriage, **St. Andrew Parish (RC)**)

Jane Garrett (daughter):

Residence - 40 Wentworth Place - June 1, 1889

Patrick Short, son of Edward Short (son-in-law):

Residence - 27 Lower O'Connell Street - June 1, 1889

Wedding Witnesses:

Pierce Short & Catherine Croghan

- Arthur Garrett & Unknown

  o Dixon Garrett & Sarah Abraham – 3 Feb 1864 (Marriage, **St. Peter Parish**)

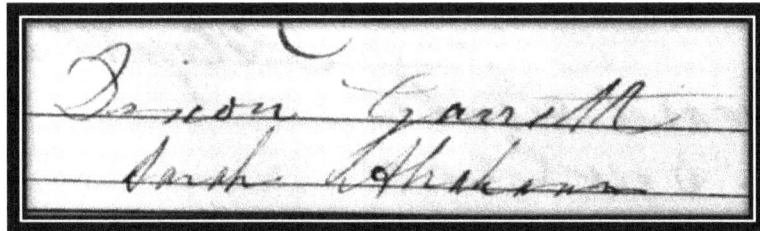

Signatures:

Dixon Garrett (son):

Residence - Roscrea, Roscrea Parish, Co. Tipperary - February 3, 1864

Occupation - Draper's Assistant - February 3, 1864

Sarah Abraham, daughter of Edward Abraham (daughter-in-law):

Residence - Kenilworth Terrace, Rathmines - February 3, 1864

Hurst

Edward Abraham (father):

    Occupation - Land Steward

Arthur Garrett (father):

    Occupation - Farmer

Wedding Witnesses:

W. C. Eggers & Anne Isdell

Signatures:

- Charles Garrett & Ellen Burke
  - Patrick Garrett – bapt. 19 Mar 1839 (Baptism, **Caharagh Parish (RC)**)

Charles Garrett (father):

    Residence - Caulbey - March 19, 1839

- Charles Garrett & Ellen Mahon
  - Ellen Mary Garrett – bapt. 1892 (Baptism, **St. Andrew Parish (RC)**)

Charles Garrett (father):

    Residence - 44 Clarendon Street - 1892

Garrett Surname Ireland: 1600s to 1900s

- Charles Garrett & Susan Marsh

  o Gulielmo Garrett – bapt. 26 Apr 1877 (Baptism, **St. Mary, Haddington Road Parish (RC)**)

Charles Garrett (father):

Residence - Pigeon House Fort - April 26, 1877

- Charles Francis Garrett & Elizabeth Jane Garrett

  o Violet Helen Garrett – b. 22 Apr 1900, bapt. 17 May 1900 (Baptism, **North Strand Parish**)

Charles Francis Garrett (father):

Residence - 12 Summerhill Parade - May 17, 1900

Occupation - Lighthouse Keeper - May 17, 1900

- Christopher Garrett & Anne Unknown

  o Thomas Garrett – bapt. 4 Nov 1765 (Baptism, **St. Catherine Parish**)

  o Samuel Garrett – bapt. 16 Mar 1767 (Baptism, **St. Catherine Parish**)

Christopher Garrett (father):

Residence - Marrow Bone Lane - November 4, 1765

Meath Street - March 16, 1767

- Daniel Garrett & Sarah Garrett

  o Richard Garrett – bapt. 21 Sep 1766 (Baptism, **St. Mary Parish**)

  o William Garrett – bapt. 19 Feb 1768 (Baptism, **St. Mary Parish**)

  o Sarah Garrett – bapt. 21 Feb 1769 (Baptism, **St. Mary, Pro Cathedral Parish (RC)**)

Hurst

Daniel Garrett (father):

Residence - Jervis Street - September 21, 1766

February 19, 1768

- David Garrett & Ellen Brien

  - Michael Garrett – bapt. 3 Oct 1825 (Baptism, **Cork - South Parish (RC)**)

- Edmond Garrett & Unknown

  - William Garrett – b. 4 Aug 1691, bapt. 4 Aug 1691 (Baptism, **St. Catherine Parish**)

  - Jane Garrett – bapt. 10 Jul 1698 (Baptism, **St. Catherine Parish**)

- Edward Garrett & Margaret Lewis

  - Margaret Garrett – bapt. 11 Mar 1830 (Baptism, **Kinsale Parish (RC)**)

Edward Garrett (father):

Residence - Camp Hill - March 11, 1830

- Edward Garrett & Margaret Unknown

  - Anne Garrett – bapt. 26 Jul 1818 (Baptism, **St. Nicholas Within Parish**)

  - Anne Garrett – bapt. 15 Dec 1822 (Baptism, **St. John Parish**)

- Edward Stephen Garrett & Unknown

Signature:

Garrett Surname Ireland: 1600s to 1900s

     ○   Henry George Garrett & Harriet Elizabeth Hill – 9 Jan 1872 (Marriage, **St. Thomas Parish**)

Signature:

Signatures (Marriage):

- Evelyn Harriett Garret – b. 15 May 1874, bapt. 2 Jul 1874 (Baptism, **St. Barnabas Parish**)

- Edward Abraham Garret – b. 9 Dec 1875, bapt. 2 Jan 1876 (Baptism, **St. Barnabas Parish**)

- Susan Mary Amelia Garrett – b. 31 Oct 1877, bapt. 15 Nov 1877 (Baptism, **St. Barnabas Parish**)

- George Charles William Garrett – b. 23 Sep 1882, bapt. 8 Oct 1882 (Baptism, **North Strand Parish**)

- Georgina Elizabeth Garrett – b. 29 Dec 1886, bapt. 30 Jan 1887 (Baptism, **North Strand Parish**)

Hurst

Henry George Garrett (son):

Residence - 3 Monks Cottage - January 9, 1872

6 Marshall Terrace, North Strand - July 2, 1874

7 Monk's Cottages - January 2, 1876

Kirt [Hard to Read] Light - November 15, 1877

47 Charleville Avenue - October 8, 1882

39 Clonliffe Road - January 30, 1887

Occupation - Custom House Officer - January 9, 1872

Light Keeper - July 2, 1874

January 2, 1876

November 15, 1877

Principal Light Keeper, Port Docks Board - October 8, 1882

Principal Light Keeper - January 30, 1887

Harriet Elizabeth Hill, daughter of Abraham Hill (daughter-in-law):

Residence - 3 Monks Cottage - January 9, 1872

Abraham Hill (father):

Occupation - Mariner

Edward Stephen Garrett (father):

Occupation - Coast Guard

Garrett Surname Ireland: 1600s to 1900s

Wedding Witnesses:

James Hewson & Georgina Grenet

Signatures:

- o William Garrett & Harriet Carr – 12 Sep 1875 (Marriage, **St. Barnabas Parish**)

Signatures:

William Garrett (father):

Residence - 12 Florence Place - September 12, 1875

Occupation - Seaman - September 12, 1875

Harriet Carr, daughter of Samuel Carr (daughter-in-law):

Residence - Coast Guard, Ring's End - September 12, 1875

Samuel Carr (father):

Occupation - Chief Officer, Coast Guards

Hurst

Edward Stephen Garrett (father):

Occupation - Seaman

Wedding Witnesses:

E. F. Garrett & Charles Carr

Signatures:

- o Benjamin Thomas Garrett & Mary Edith Donovan – 17 Dec 1876 (Marriage, **St. Barnabas Parish**)

Signatures:

- ▪ Edward Alexander Francis Garrett – b. 28 Oct 1877, bapt. 2 Dec 1877 (Baptism, **St. Barnabas Parish**)

Benjamin Thomas Garrett (son):

Residence - 9 Coburgh Place, Dublin - December 17, 1876

13 George's Place, Kingstown - December 2, 1877

Garrett Surname Ireland: 1600s to 1900s

Occupation - Seaman - December 17, 1876

December 2, 1877

Mary Edith Donovan, daughter of Edwin Alexander Donovan (daughter-in-law):

Residence - 1 North Dock Street - December 17, 1876

Relationship Status at Marriage - minor

Edwin Alexander Donovan (father):

Signature:

Occupation - Agriculturalist

Edward Stephen Garret (father):

Occupation - Seaman

Wedding Witnesses:

Edwin Alexander Donovan & Edward Stephen Garrett

Signatures:

Hurst

○ John Francis Garrett (1st Marriage) & Catherine Griffin, d. bef. Mar 1887 – 26 Jul 1880

(Marriage, **St. Anne Parish**)

Signatures:

▪ Mary Amelia Garrett – b. 21 Jan 1884, bapt. 10 Feb 1884 (Baptism, **St. Barnabas Parish**)

▪ Edward Christopher Garrett – b. 16 Jun 1881, bapt. 30 Mar 1887 (Baptism, **North Strand**

Parish)

John Francis Garrett (son):

Residence - 2 Malacca Place, North Wall, Dublin - July 26, 1880

6 Guilfort Terrace, North Strand - February 10, 1884

9 Bayview Avenue - March 30, 1887

Occupation - Light Keeper - July 26, 1880

February 10, 1884

March 30, 1887

Catherine Griffin, daughter of Patrick Griffin (daughter-in-law):

Residence - 14 Duke Street - July 26, 1880

32 Birksley Road, Dublin - July 26, 1880

Garrett Surname Ireland: 1600s to 1900s

Patrick Griffin (father):

    Occupation - Tailor

Edward Stephen Garrett (father):

    Occupation - Navy

Wedding Witnesses:

Thomas Nooney & Susan Murray

Signatures:

- o John Francis Garrett (2nd Marriage) & Elizabeth Jane Cain – 2 Mar 1887 (Marriage, **St. Mary Parish**)

Signatures:

- John Francis Garrett – b. 1 Aug 1888, bapt. 26 Aug 1888 (Baptism, **North Strand Parish**)

- Elizabeth Jane Sarah Garrett – b. 25 Jul 1890, bapt. 10 Aug 1890 (Baptism, **North Strand Parish**)

0
Hurst

- Henry Charles Garrett – b. 11 Mar 1892, bapt. 3 Apr 1892 (Baptism, **North Strand Parish**)

- Emily Amelia Garrett – b. 4 Sep 1894, bapt. 14 Oct 1894 (Baptism, **North Strand Parish**)

- Victoria Eleanor Garrett – b. 4 Apr 1897, bapt. 6 May 1897 (Baptism, **North Strand Parish**)

John Francis Garrett (son):

Residence - 9 Bayview Avenue - March 2, 1887

3 James Street - August 26, 1888

3 James Street, North Strand - August 10, 1890

35 Strandville Avenue - April 3, 1892

October 14, 1894

May 6, 1897

Occupation - Light Keeper - March 2, 1887

August 26, 1888

August 10, 1890

April 3, 1892

October 14, 1894

May 6, 1897

Relationship Status at 2nd Marriage - widow

0

Elizabeth Jane Cain, daughter of Matthew Cain (2nd wife) (daughter-in-law):

Residence - 44 Rutland Square - March 2, 1887

Matthew Cain (father):

Occupation - Navy Pensioner

Edward Stephen Garrett (father):

Occupation - Navy Pensioner

Wedding Witnesses:

George Thomas & Mary J. Poulton

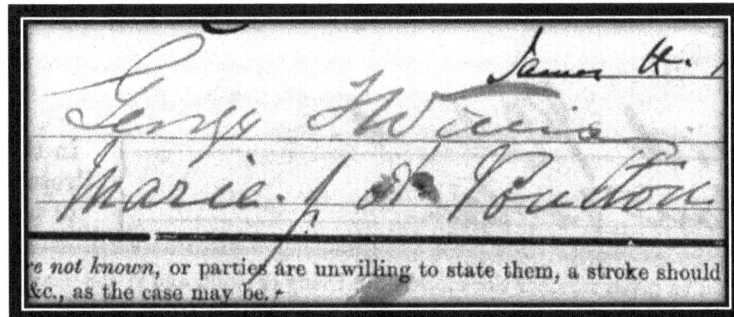

Signatures:

- George Garrett & Catherine Kane
  - John Garrett – b. 1873, bapt. 1873 (Baptism, **Chapelizod Parish (RC)**)
  - Mary Elizabeth Garrett – b. 5 Jun 1875, bapt. 21 Jun 1875 (Baptism, **St. Michan Parish (RC)**)

George Garrett (father):

Residence - Chapelizod - 1873

205 Phibsboro - June 21, 1875

Hurst

- George Garrett & Elizabeth Garrett

  o George Garrett – b. 14 Jan 1823, bapt. 23 Feb 1823 (Baptism, **St. Mary Parish**)

George Garrett (father):

Residence - 26 Britain Street - February 23, 1823

- George Garrett & Elizabeth Unknown

  o Bartholomew Garrett – bapt. 17 Apr 1796 (Baptism, **St. Catherine Parish**)

George Garrett (father):

Residence - No. 14 Thomas Street - April 17, 1796

- George Garrett & Joan Allen

  o Martha Roseanne Garrett – b. 1855, bapt. 1855 (Baptism, **Chapelizod Parish (RC)**)

  o Arthur Michael Garrett – b. 7 Sep 1868, bapt. 1 Oct 1868 (Baptism, **St. James Parish (RC)**)

George Garrett (father):

Residence - Inchicore Railway Works, James Street - 1855

Inchicore - October 1, 1868

- George Garrett & Mary Mulroney

  o Mary Garrett – bapt 21 Dec 1840 or 24 Dec 1841(Baptism, **St. Michan Parish (RC)**)

  o Mary Garrett, bapt. 21 Dec 1840 or 24 Dec 1841 (Baptism, **St. Michan Parish (RC)**) & Stephen Fitzsimons – 14 Apr 1861 (Marriage, **St. Mary, Pro Cathedral Parish (RC)**)

    ▪ Joseph William Fitzsimons – b. 9 May 1866, bapt. 11 May 1866 (Baptism, **St. Michan Parish (RC)**)

- Christopher Fitzsimons – b. 27 Dec 1868, bapt. 8 Jan 1869 (Baptism, **St. Mary, Pro Cathedral Parish** (RC))

- William Fitzsimons – b. 28 Oct 1870, bapt. 7 Nov 1870 (Baptism, **St. Mary, Pro Cathedral Parish** (RC))

- William Fitzsimons – b. 26 Dec 1871, bapt. 3 Jan 1872 (Baptism, **St. Mary, Pro Cathedral Parish** (RC))

Mary Garrett (daughter):

Residence - 72 Capel Street - April 14, 1861

Stephen Fitzsimons, son of Andrew Fitzsimons & Catherine Fitzsimons

(son-in-law):

Residence - 14 Boot Lane - April 14, 1861

65 Mary's Lane - May 11, 1866

East Arran Street - January 8, 1869

31 East Arran Street - November 7, 1870

98 East Arran Street - January 3, 1872

Wedding Witnesses:

John Flanagan & Mary Fitzsimons

- ○ William Garrett, bapt. 1 Aug 1843 (Baptism, **St. Michan Parish** (RC)) & Catherine Fisher – 21 Jan 1866 (Marriage, **St. Andrew Parish** (RC))

  - Joseph Garrett – b. 1868, bapt. 1868 (Baptism, **St. Andrew Parish** (RC))

  - John Thomas Garrett – b. 1869, bapt. 1869 (Baptism, **St. Andrew Parish** (RC))

Hurst

- Mary Garrett – b. 1871, bapt. 1872 (Baptism, **St. Andrew Parish** (RC))

- Elizabeth Garrett – b. 1874, bapt. 1874 (Baptism, **St. Andrew Parish** (RC))

- William Garrett – b. 1875, bapt. 1875 (Baptism, **St. Andrew Parish** (RC))

- James Garrett – b. 1877, bapt. 1877 (Baptism, **St. Andrew Parish** (RC))

- Michael Garrett – b. 27 Sep 1878, bapt. 30 Sep 1878 (Baptism, **St. Mary, Pro Cathedral Parish** (RC))

- Louise Garrett – b. 6 Mar 1880, bapt. 10 Mar 1880 (Baptism, **St. Mary, Pro Cathedral Parish** (RC))

- Patrick Garrett – b. 23 Oct 1881, bapt. 2 Nov 1881 (Baptism, **St. Mary, Pro Cathedral Parish** (RC))

- Isabel Garrett – b. 17 Sep 1883, bapt. 26 Sep 1883 (Baptism, **St. Mary, Pro Cathedral Parish** (RC))

- Henry Christopher Garrett – b. 15 Mar 1886, bapt. 24 Mar 1886 (Baptism, **St. Mary, Pro Cathedral Parish** (RC))

William Garrett (son):

Residence - 4 Windmill Lane - January 21, 1866

Quay - 1868

109 Townsend Street - 1869

1872

1874

1875

1877

59 Lower Dominick Street - September 30, 1878

September 26, 1883

59 Dominick Lane - March 10, 1880

November 2, 1881

March 24, 1886

Catherine Fisher, daughter of John Fisher & Mary Unknown (daughter-in-law):

Residence - 4 Windmill Lane - January 21, 1866

Wedding Witnesses:

James Fisher & Mary Connor

- ○ Sarah Garrett – bapt. 2 Jan 1846 (Baptism, St. Michan Parish (RC))

- ○ Anne Garrett – bapt. Mar 1848 (Baptism, St. Michan Parish (RC))

- ○ Louise Garrett, bapt. Dec 1849 (Baptism, St. Michan Parish (RC)) & James Cooke – 12 Jan 1873 (Marriage, St. Michan Parish (RC))

  - ▪ James Cooke – b. 12 Oct 1873, bapt. 15 Oct 1873 (Baptism, St. Mary, Pro Cathedral Parish (RC))

  - ▪ Patrick Cooke – b. 15 Mar 1875, bapt. 19 Mar 1875 (Baptism, St. Mary, Pro Cathedral Parish (RC))

Louise Garrett (daughter):

Residence - 37 Arran Street - January 12, 1873

James Cooke, son of Michael Cooke & Mary Unknown (son-in-law):

Residence - 25 Britain Street - January 12, 1873

Hurst

31 East Arran Street - October 15, 1873

30 East Arran Street - March 19, 1875

Wedding Witnesses:

James Mooney & Bridget Mooney

- o Sarah Garrett, bapt. 24 Oct 1851 (Baptism, **St. Michan Parish (RC)**) & James Fitzgibbon – 3 Jul 1876 (Marriage, **St. Mary, Pro Cathedral Parish (RC)**)

  - ▪ Catherine Fitzgibbon, b. 14 Jan 1876, bapt. 24 Jan 1876 (Baptism, **St. Mary, Pro Cathedral Parish (RC)**) & Patrick Higgins – 1 Jul 1899 (Marriage, **St. Mary, Pro Cathedral Parish (RC)**)

Catherine Fitzgibbon (daughter):

Residence - 30 East Arran Street - January 24, 1876

4 Hill Street - July 1, 1899

Patrick Higgins, son of Edward Higgins & Mary Kinsella (son-in-law):

Residence - 4 Hill Street - July 1, 1899

Wedding Witnesses:

Joseph Kenahan & Mary Flynn

- ▪ Christopher Joseph Fitzgibbon – b. 26 Dec 1877, bapt. 7 Jan 1878 (Baptism, **St. Mary, Pro Cathedral Parish (RC)**)

- ▪ Joseph Fitzgibbon – b. 15 Oct 1881, bapt. 26 Oct 1881 (Baptism, **St. Mary, Pro Cathedral Parish (RC)**)

Sarah Garrett (daughter):

Residence - 31 East Arran Street - July 3, 1876

James Fitzgibbon, son of Patrick Fitzgibbon & Mary Unknown (son-in-law):

Residence - 5 Sackville Place - July 3, 1876

20 Montgomery Street - January 7, 1878

2 Nerney's Court - October 26, 1881

Wedding Witnesses:

John Lyons & Catherine Fitzgibbon

- George Garrett & Unknown
  - Isabel Garrett & William Smyth – 19 Apr 1849 (Marriage, **St. Peter Parish**)

Signatures:

Isabel Garrett (daughter):

Residence - Kensington Terrace, Rathmines - April 19, 1849

William Smyth, son of John Smyth (son-in-law):

Residence - Black Rock, Booterstown Parish - April 19, 1849

Occupation - Clerk in Boot Office - April 19, 1849

Hurst

John Smyth (father):

    Occupation - Soldier

George Garrett (father):

    Occupation - Surgeon in Army

Wedding Witnesses:

John Garrett & George Garrett

Signatures:

- George Garrett & Unknown
  - George Garrett & Susan Woods – 20 Apr 1852 (Marriage, **St. Mark Parish**)

Signatures:

Garrett Surname Ireland: 1600s to 1900s

- George Garrett, b. 1858, bapt. 1858 (Baptism, **St. Andrew Parish (RC)**) & Frances Mitchell – 6 Feb 1890 (Marriage, **St. Mary, Pro Cathedral Parish (RC)**)

George Garrett (son):

Residence - 2 Grenville Place - February 6, 1890

Frances Mitchell, daughter of Patrick Mitchell & Frances Malone

(daughter-in-law):

Residence - 2 Grenville Place - February 6, 1890

Wedding Witnesses:

James Lee & Elizabeth Lee

- David Garrett – b. 1860, bapt. 1860 (Baptism, **St. Andrew Parish (RC)**)
- Catherine Garrett – b. 2 Oct 1868, bapt. 4 Oct 1868 (Baptism, **Rotunda Chapel Parish**) (Baptism, **St. Mary Parish**)
- Richard Joseph Garrett – bapt. 1892 (Baptism, **St. Andrew Parish (RC)**)

George Garrett (son):

Residence - Townsend Street - April 20, 1852

20 Stephen Street - 1858

7 Adams Court - 1860

15 Andrew's Lane - October 4, 1868

44 Clarendon Street - 1892

Hurst

Occupation - Ivory Turner - April 20, 1852

Turner - October 4, 1868

Susan Woods, daughter of James Woods (daughter-in-law):

Residence - Townsend Street - April 20, 1852

James Woods (father):

Occupation - House Painter

George Garrett (father):

Occupation - Harness Maker

Wedding Witnesses:

James Woods & Edward Fox

Signatures:

24

- George Garrett & Unknown

Signatures:

o John Galloway Garrett & Elizabeth Margaret Bradshaw – 11 Jul 1878 (Marriage, **Clontarf**

Parish)

Signatures:

- Mary Elizabeth Anne Garrett – b. 10 Jul 1879, bapt. 14 Aug 1879 (Baptism, **Clontarf**

Parish)

- Clare Henrietta Hall Garrett – b. 18 Mar 1887, bapt. 9 Jun 1887 (Baptism, **Clontarf**

Parish)

John Galloway Garrett (son):

Residence - Clontarf - July 11, 1878

August 14, 1879

Hurst

Trinity College Ceylon - June 9, 1887

Occupation - Clerk in Holy Orders - July 11, 1878

June 9, 1887

Clerk - August 14, 1879

Elizabeth Margaret Bradshaw, daughter of M. Bradshaw (daughter-in-law):

Residence - Clontarf - July 11, 1878

M. Bradshaw (father):

Occupation - Clerk

George Garrett (father):

Occupation - Clerk

Wedding Witnesses:

George H. Garrett & Henry Hall Bradshaw

Signatures:

Garrett Surname Ireland: 1600s to 1900s

○ Emily Marian Garrett & Francis Bernard (B e r n a r d) Lawson – 5 Dec 1883 (Marriage, Leeson Park Parish)

Signatures:

Emily Marian Garrett (daughter):

Residence - Kelmeaque Road - December 5, 1883

Francis Bernard Lawson, son of George Gray Lawson (son-in-law):

Residence - Northampton - December 5, 1883

Occupation - Lieutenant H M Northampton Shire Regiment - December 5, 1883

George Gray Lawson (father):

Occupation - Clergyman

George Garrett (father):

Occupation - Clergyman

Wedding Witnesses:

E. Brereton & George Garrett

Signatures:

Hurst

○ George Henry St. P. Garrett & Helen Walker Greer – 12 Sep 1888 (Marriage, **Leeson Park Parish**)

Signatures:

Signatures (Marriage):

George Henry St. P. Garrett (son):

Residence - Wisden Rectory, Lancashire - September 12, 1888

18 Burlington Road, Dublin - September 12, 1888

Occupation - Clergyman of Church of England - September 12, 1888

Helen Walker Greer, daughter of Robert Greer (daughter-in-law):

Residence - 15 Raglan Road - September 12, 1888

Occupation - Lady - September 12, 1888

Robert Greer (father):

Occupation - Gentleman

George Garrett (father):

Occupation - Clergyman Church of Ireland

Wedding Witnesses:

Edward St. Greer & K. H. Mills

Signatures:

- George Garrett & Unknown
  - Richard Garrett & Ellen McCormack (M c C o r m a c k) – 29 Nov 1886 (Marriage, St. Thomas Parish)

Signatures:

- Susan Garrett – b. 1887, bapt. 1892 (Baptism, St. Andrew Parish (RC))

Hurst

Richard Garrett (son):

Residence - 7 Mail Borough Place - November 29, 1886

12 Pitt Street - 1892

Occupation - Valet - November 29, 1886

Ellen McCormack, daughter of Charles McCormack (daughter-in-law):

Residence - 46 Tyrone Street - November 29, 1886

Charles McCormack (father):

Occupation - Printer

George Garrett (father):

Occupation - Carver

Wedding Witnesses:

Ellen McCormack & George Garrett

Signatures:

Garrett Surname Ireland: 1600s to 1900s

- Harold Garrett & Harriet Garrett
  - William Henry Garrett – b. 6 May 1896, bapt. 4 Jun 1896 (Baptism, **St. Peter Parish**)

Harold Garrett (father):

Residence - 21 Upper Digge Street - June 4, 1896

Occupation - Soldier - June 4, 1896

- Henry Garrett & Unknown
  - Henry Bold Garrett & Maude Kathleen Sprabrook – Unclear (Baptism, **Sandford Parish**)

Henry Bold Garrett (son):

Residence - Aranmore, Mina Road, Monkstown - Unclear

Occupation - Medical Doctor - Unclear

Maude Kathleen Sprabrook, daughter of Nicholas Sprabrook (daughter-in-law):

Residence - Woodstock, Sandyford Road - Unclear

Nicholas Sprabrook (father):

Occupation - Esquire

Henry Garrett (father):

Occupation - Bank Manager

Wedding Witnesses:

J. H. Stewart & Mary L. Garrett

Hurst

- Henry Lloyd Perrier Garrett & Unknown

  o Henry Lloyd Perrier Garrett & Mary Amelia Hill – 26 Dec 1887 (Marriage, **St. Barnabas Parish**)

Signatures:

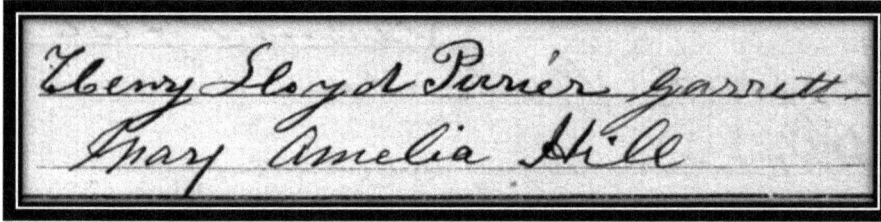

  ▪ Caroline Amelia Garrett – b. 25 May 1889, bapt. 21 Jul 1889 (Baptism, **St. Barnabas Parish**)

Henry Lloyd Perrier Garrett (son):

Residence - 18 Upper Oriel Street - December 26, 1887

July 21, 1889

Occupation - Mariner - December 26, 1887

Seaman - July 21, 1889

Mary Amelia Hill, daughter of Abraham Hill (daughter-in-law):

Residence - 15 Upper Oriel Street - December 26, 1887

Abraham Hill (father):

Occupation - Seaman

Henry Lloyd Perrier Garrett (father):

Occupation - Rope Maker

Garrett Surname Ireland: 1600s to 1900s

Wedding Witnesses:

Robert Hill & Margaret Wilson

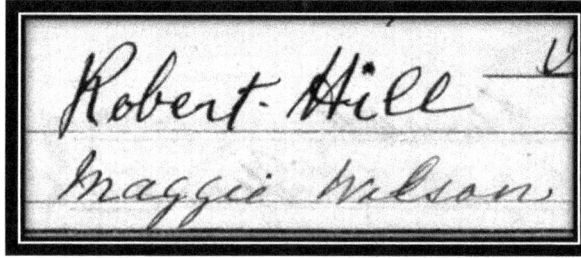

Signatures:

- Ignatius Garrett & Sarah Unknown

  - Elizabeth Garrett – bapt. 3 Jun 1746 (Baptism, **St. Nicholas Parish** (RC))

- James Garrett & Agnes Hunt

  - James Joseph Garrett – b. 2 Mar 1881, bapt. 14 Mar 1881 (Baptism, **St. Mary, Pro Cathedral Parish** (RC))

James Garrett (father):

Residence - 22 Green Street - March 14, 1881

- James Garrett & Catherine Garrett

  - Elizabeth Garrett – bapt. 3 May 1795 (Baptism, **St. Paul Parish**)

- James Garrett & Catherine Sullivan

  - John Garrett – bapt. 7 Jul 1852 (Baptism, **Clontead Parish** (RC))

  - Michael Garrett – bapt. 20 Apr 1854 (Baptism, **Clontead Parish** (RC))

- James Garrett & Catherine Unknown

  - Mary Garrett – bapt. 29 Oct 1758 (Baptism, **St. Audoen Parish**)

Hurst

- James Garrett & Cecelia Unknown

  - Judith Garrett – bapt. 26 May 1747 (Baptism, **St. Catherine Parish** (RC))

  - James Garrett – bapt. 1752 (Baptism, **St. Andrew Parish** (RC))

- James Garrett & Eleanor Unknown

  - William Garrett – bapt. 8 May 1758 (Baptism, **St. Catherine Parish** (RC))

- James Garrett & Elizabeth Garrett

  - Catherine Garrett – bapt. 8 Apr 1741 (Baptism, **St. Catherine Parish** (RC))

- James Garrett & Elizabeth Unknown

  - William Garrett – bapt. 9 Feb 1750 (Baptism, **St. Catherine Parish** (RC))

  - Catherine Garrett – bapt. 6 Oct 1754 (Baptism, **St. Catherine Parish** (RC))

- James Garrett & Emily Cruise

  - Mary Anne Garrett – bapt. 1777 (Baptism, **SS. Michael & John Parish** (RC))

- James Garrett & Jane Beatty

  - Mary Jane Garrett & John Kennedy – 5 Jul 1870 (Marriage, **St. Lawrence Parish** (RC))

    - John Kennedy – b. 8 Apr 1873, bapt. 12 May 1873 (Baptism, **St. Lawrence Parish** (RC))

    - Joseph Kennedy – b. 1 Jul 1874, bapt. 10 Jul 1874 (Baptism, **St. Mary, Pro Cathedral Parish** (RC))

    - Mary Jane Kennedy – b. 12 Jan 1877, bapt. 16 Feb 1877 (Baptism, **St. Mary, Pro Cathedral Parish** (RC))

Mary Jane Garrett (daughter):

Residence - 114 Amiens Street - July 5, 1870

John Kennedy, son of Daniel Kennedy & Mary Darcy (son-in-law):

Residence - Unclear - July 5, 1870

Garrett Surname Ireland: 1600s to 1900s

114 Amiens Street - May 12, 1873

4 Northumberland Square - July 10, 1874

Aldboro Barracks - February 16, 1877

Wedding Witnesses:

Richard Walsh & Mary Anne Donnelly

- James Garrett & Jane England

  o Mary Anne Garrett – bapt. 11 Jan 1809 (Baptism, **Cork - SS. Peter & Paul Parish** (RC))

- James Garrett & Margaret Coleman

  o Honor Garrett – bapt. 23 Feb 1858 (Baptism, **Clontead Parish** (RC))

- James Garrett & Mary Garrett

  o John Garrett – bur. 25 Oct 1749 (Burial, **St. Luke Parish**)

  o James Garrett – bapt. 14 May 1756 (Baptism, **St. Luke Parish**)

  o Mary Garrett – bapt. 29 Oct 1758 (Baptism, **St. Audoen Parish**)

- James Garrett & Mary Garrett

  o Mary Jane Garrett – b. 15 Mar 1882, bapt. 10 May 1882 (Baptism, **St. George Parish**)

James Garrett (father):

Residence - Hutton's Lane - May 10, 1882

Occupation - Game Keeper - May 10, 1882

Hurst

- James Garrett & Mary Unknown

  - John Garrett – bapt. 3 Oct 1748 (Baptism, **St. Nicholas Without Parish**)

James Garrett (father):

Residence - Coombe - October 3, 1748

- James Garrett & Mary Anne Garrett

  - Arthur James Garrett – bapt. 4 Feb 1855 (Baptism, **Arbour Hill Barracks Parish**)

James Garrett (father):

Occupation - Private, 3rd Dragoon Guards - February 4, 1855

- James Garrett & Penelope Garrett

  - Jane Garrett – bapt. 4 Nov 1722 (Baptism, **St. Mary Parish**)

- James Garrett & Thomason Unknown

  - Mary Garrett – bapt. 6 Nov 1748 (Baptism, **St. Michan Parish (RC)**)

- James Garrett & Unknown

  - Catherine Garrett – bapt. 21 May 1660 (Baptism, **St. Michan Parish**)

- James Garrett & Unknown – 10 Aug 1766 (Marriage, **St. Catherine Parish (RC)**)

- James Garrett & Unknown

  - George Garrett & Ellen Walker – 17 Jun 1854 (Marriage, **St. Mary Parish**)

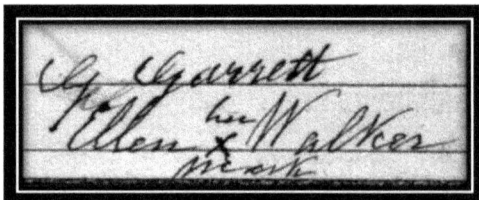

Signatures:

Garrett Surname Ireland: 1600s to 1900s

George Garrett (son):

    Residence - Liversdale Barracks - June 17, 1854

    Occupation - Printer, 63rd Regiment - June 17, 1854

Ellen Walker, daughter of James Walker (daughter-in-law):

    Residence - 25 Caple Street - June 17, 1854

James Walker (father):

    Occupation - Blacksmith

James Garrett (father):

    Occupation - Laborer

Wedding Witnesses:

W. Carrick & Jane Walker

Signatures:

- James Garrett & Unknown
  - James Garrett & Anne Bowler Lawrence – 22 Nov 1870 (Marriage, **St. Peter Parish**)

Signatures:

Hurst

James Garrett (son):

    Residence - 18 Harcourt Road - November 22, 1870

    Occupation - Domestic Servant - November 22, 1870

    Relationship Status at Marriage - widow

Anne Bowler Lawrence, daughter of George Bowler (daughter-in-law):

    Residence - 18 Harcourt Road - November 22, 1870

    Relationship Status at Marriage - widow

George Bowler (father):

    Occupation - Broom Maker

James Garrett (father):

    Occupation - Farmer

Wedding Witnesses:

Elizabeth Garrett & George Prescott

Signatures:

- James Perkins Garrett & Christine Armitage (A r m i t a g e) E. Garrett

Signatures:

  o Priscilla Cecelia Garrett & John Winter Humphrys – 15 Feb 1854 (Marriage, **Carlow**

    Parish)

Signatures:

Priscilla Cecelia Garret (daughter):

  Residence - Evington, Carlow - February 15, 1854

  Relationship Status at Marriage - minor

Hurst

John Winter Humphrys, son of William Humphrys (son-in-law):

    Residence - Ballyhouse House, Co. Cavan - February 15, 1854

    Occupation - Gentleman - February 15, 1854

William Humphrys (father):

    Occupation - Gentleman

James Perkins Garrett (father):

    Occupation - Clergyman

Wedding Witnesses:

Unknown Annesley & H. Annesley

Signatures:

- o James Hugh Moore Garrett & Isabel Sarah Maxwell – 11 Apr 1894 (Marriage, **St. Stephen Parish**)

Signatures:

Garrett Surname Ireland: 1600s to 1900s

James Hugh Moore Garrett (son):

 Residence - Hotel Metropole, Dublin - April 11, 1894

 Corriewood, Castle Wellan - April 11, 1894

 Occupation - Esquire - April 11, 1894

 Relationship Status at Marriage - widow

Isabel Sarah Maxwell, daughter of Richard Maxwell (daughter-in-law):

 Residence - 96 Lower Baggot Street - April 11, 1894

 Fortland, Mount Nugent - April 11, 1894

Richard Maxwell (father):

 Occupation - Honorable

James Perkins Garrett (father):

 Occupation - Clerk in Holy Orders

Wedding Witnesses:

Somerset H. Maxwell & Anne T. Burrowes

Signatures:

- o Sylvia Christina Armitage (A r m i t a g e) Garrett – b. 12 Mar 1853, bapt. 1 May 1853 (Baptism, **Painestown Parish**)

- o Harriet Caroline Garrett – b. 31 May Unclear, bapt. 25 Jun Unclear (Baptism, **Painestown Parish**)

- John Garrett & Batty Keefe

  - o David Garrett – bapt. Oct 1823 (Baptism, **Clontead Parish (RC)**)

- John Garrett & Bridget McGuire – 17 Nov 1777 (Marriage, **St. Audoen Parish**) (Baptism, **St. Audoen Parish (RC)**)

Wedding Witnesses:

Charles Carter, William Lucas, Margaret Dalton, & Mary McLane

- John Garrett & Bridget Garrett

  - o Elizabeth Garrett – bapt. 13 Oct 1746 (Baptism, **St. Catherine Parish (RC)**)

- John Garrett & Catherine Garrett

  - o John Garrett – bapt. 17 Nov 1717 (Baptism, **St. Luke Parish**)

John Garrett (father):

Residence - Lower Coombe - November 17, 1717

Occupation - Wier Drawer - November 17, 1717

- John Garrett & Catherine Hihily

  - o Honor Garrett – bapt. 8 Oct 1798 (Baptism, **Bantry Parish (RC)**)

- John Garrett & Elizabeth Unknown

  - o Elizabeth Garrett – bapt. 10 Oct 1767 (Baptism, **St. Nicholas Parish (RC)**)

Garrett Surname Ireland: 1600s to 1900s

- John Garrett & Elizabeth Unknown

  - George Thomas Garrett – b. 7 Jun 1852, bapt. 27 Jun 1852 (Baptism, **St. James Parish**)

  - Mary Jane Garrett – b. 4 Dec 1853, bapt. 25 Dec 1853 (Baptism, **St. James Parish**)

  - Elizabeth Garrett – b. 1 Jan 1857, bapt. 15 Feb 1857 (Baptism, **St. James Parish**)

  - Eleanor Garrett – b. 13 Apr 1862, bapt. 20 Apr 1862 (Baptism, **St. Jude Parish**)

  - Henry John Garrett – b. 30 May 1870, bapt. 3 Jul 1870 (Baptism, **St. Jude Parish**)

John Garrett (father):

Residence - Inchicore - June 27, 1852

April 20, 1862

July 3, 1870

5 North Inchicore - December 25, 1853

5 North Inchicore Terrace - February 15, 1857

Occupation - Engine Owner - June 27, 1852

Engine Driver - December 25, 1853

February 15, 1857

April 20, 1862

July 3, 1870

- John Garrett & Ellen Dempsey

  - John Garrett – b. 25 May 1891, bapt. 5 Jun 1891 (Baptism, **St. Mary, Pro Cathedral Parish** (RC))

Hurst

John Garrett (father):

Residence - Rotunda - June 5, 1891

- John Garrett & Ellen Noonan

  - Inna Garrett – bapt. 17 Mar 1839 (Baptism, **Clontead Parish (RC)**)

  - John Garrett – bapt. 29 Mar 1841 (Baptism, **Clontead Parish (RC)**)

- John Garrett & Frances Garrett

  - Bridget Garrett – bapt. 20 Feb 1825 (Baptism, **St. Paul Parish**)

- John Garrett & Henrica Unknown

  - Mary Garrett – bapt. 21 Jul 1817 (Baptism, **St. Michan Parish (RC)**)

- John Garrett & Honor O'Brien

  - Mary Garrett – bapt. 28 Apr 1831 (Baptism, **Cork - South Parish (RC)**)

  - Anne Garrett – bapt. 15 Nov 1832 (Baptism, **Cork - South Parish (RC)**)

  - Francis Garrett – bapt. Jul 1834 (Baptism, **Cork - South Parish (RC)**)

- John Garrett & Honor Unknown

  - Robert Garrett – bapt. 1 Dec 1712 (Baptism, **St. Nicholas Within Parish**)

  - Rebecca Garrett – bapt. 16 Jan 1715 (Baptism, **St. Nicholas Within Parish**)

- John Garrett & Jane Deane – 20 Jan 1639 (Marriage, **St. Bride Parish**)

- John Garrett & Jane Frankling – 2 Jan 1727 (Marriage, **St. Michan Parish (RC)**)

Wedding Witnesses:

Henry Skinner & John Butterfield

- John Garrett & Jane Unknown

  - John Garrett – bur. 5 Jul 1730 (Burial, **St. Mary Parish**)

Garrett Surname Ireland: 1600s to 1900s

- John Garrett & Jane Unknown

  - Richard Garrett – bapt. 17 Dec 1740 (Baptism, **St. Catherine Parish** (RC))

  - Elizabeth Garrett – b. Dec 1740, bapt. 17 Dec 1740 (Baptism, **St. Catherine Parish** (RC))

- John Garrett & Margaret Buckley

  - Mary Garrett – bapt. 26 Mar 1826 (Baptism, **Tracton Abbey Parish** (RC))

  - Ellen Garrett – bapt. Oct 1828 (Baptism, **Tracton Abbey Parish** (RC))

- John Garrett & Margaret Garrett

  - John Garrett – bapt. 26 Aug 1722 (Baptism, **St. Catherine Parish**)

- John Garrett & Martha Unknown

  - Henry Garret – bapt. 14 Jan 1721 (Baptism, **St. Nicholas Without Parish**)

John Garrett (father):

Residence - Patrick Street - January 14, 1721

- John Garrett & Mary Bouge

  - George Garrett – bapt. May 1810 (Baptism, **Clonakilty Parish** (RC))

- John Garrett & Mary Garrett

  - James Garrett – bur. 16 Jul 1690 (Burial, **St. John Parish**)

  - Elizabeth Garrett – b. 30 Sep 1692, bapt. 2 Oct 1692 (Baptism, **St. John Parish**), bur. 11 Nov 1692 (Burial, **St. John Parish**)

  - Jane Garrett – b. 2 Jan 1694, bapt. 5 Jan 1694 (Baptism, **St. John Parish**)

  - Mary Garrett – b. 14 Jan 1695, bapt. 18 Jan 1695 (Baptism, **St. John Parish**)

  - Edward Garrett – b. 1 Jan 1697, bapt. 3 Jan 1697 (Baptism, **St. John Parish**)

  - Susan Garrett – bur. 24 Mar 1699 (Burial, **St. John Parish**)

Hurst

John Garrett (father):

Residence - Fishamble Street - January 3, 1697

- John Garrett & Mary Unknown

  o Margaret Garrett – bapt. 30 Jul 1821 (Baptism, **St. John Parish**)

John Garrett (father):

Occupation - Soldier - July 30, 1821

- John Garrett & Unknown

  o John Garrett – bur. 20 Jun 1695(Burial, **St. Audoen Parish**)

  o John Garrett – bur. 20 Apr 1700 (Burial, **St. Audoen Parish**)

- John Garrett & Unknown

  o Unknown Garrett – bur. 8 Mar 1713 (Burial, **St. Nicholas Within Parish**)

Unknown Garrett (child):

Age at Death - child

- John Garrett & Unknown

  o Alexander Charles Garrett & Leticia Hope – 29 Jun 1854 (Marriage, **St. Peter Parish**)

Signature:

Garrett Surname Ireland: 1600s to 1900s

Signatures (Marriage):

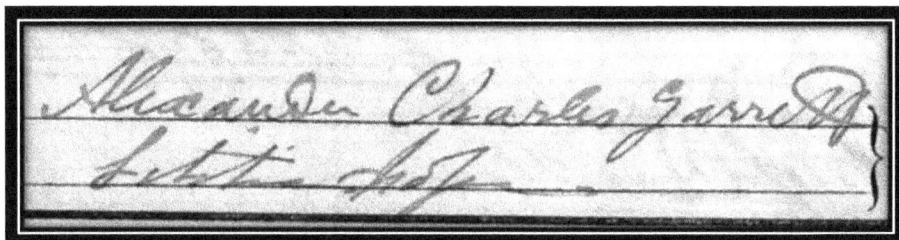

Alexander Charles Garrett (son):

    Residence - 5 Rathmines - June 29, 1854

    Occupation - Esquire - June 29, 1854

Leticia Hope, daughter of William Hope (daughter-in-law):

    Residence - 5 Rathmines - June 29, 1854

William Hope (father):

    Occupation - Solicitor

John Garrett (father):

    Occupation - Clerk in Holy Orders

Hurst

Wedding Witnesses:

William Milward Jones & Leonard Cooper

Signatures:

- John Garrett & Unknown

  - George Garrett & Ellen Smyth – 23 Jun 1865 (Marriage, **St. Peter Parish**)

Signatures:

George Garrett (son):

    Residence - Beggar's Bush Barracks - June 23, 1865

    Occupation - Private in 78th Regiment - June 23, 1865

Ellen Smyth, daughter of William Smyth (daughter-in-law):

    Residence - 9 Lower Baggot Street - June 23, 1865

William Smyth (father):

    Occupation - Farmer

Garrett Surname Ireland: 1600s to 1900s

John Garrett (father):

Occupation - Watch Glass Maker

Wedding Witnesses:

Michael Prienty & Samuel Bradley

Signatures:

- John Garrett & Unknown
  - Frederick B. Garrett & Agnes M. Fogarty – 10 Feb 1892 (Marriage, **St. Andrew Parish** (RC))

Frederick B. Garrett (son):

Residence - Lintree, Liverpool - February 10, 1892

Agnes M. Fogarty, daughter of Owen Fogarty (daughter-in-law):

Residence - Aughrim, Co. Wicklow - February 10, 1892

Wedding Witnesses:

John B. Garrett & Frances G. Fogarty

- John Farroll Garrett & Sarah Nolan – 12 May 1840 (Marriage, **St. Catherine Parish** (RC))
- Joseph Garrett & Honor Lynch
  - John Garrett – bapt. 21 May 1804 (Baptism, **Cork - South Parish** (RC))

Hurst

Joseph Garrett (father):

    Residence - Morrison's Island - May 21, 1804

- Joseph Garrett & Mary Daily – 11 Oct 1843 (Marriage, **St. Thomas Parish**)

Signatures:

Joseph Garrett (husband):

    Residence - St. Thomas Parish - October 11, 1843

Mary Daly (wife):

    Residence - St. Thomas Parish - October 11, 1843

Wedding Witnesses:

Catherine Daily & Robert Hooper

Signatures:

Garrett Surname Ireland: 1600s to 1900s

- Joseph Garrett & Sarah Garrett

  o Mary Ellen Garrett – b. 24 Jan 1861, bapt. 1 Mar 1861 (Baptism, **St. Mark Parish**)

  o Elizabeth Garrett – b. 27 Nov 1862, bapt. 21 Dec 1862 (Baptism, **St. Mark Parish**)

  o John Garrett – b. 14 Dec 1864, bapt. 22 Jan 1865 (Baptism, **St. Mark Parish**)

Joseph Garrett (father):

Residence - 20 Boyne Street - March 1, 1861

December 21, 1862

10 Boyne Street - January 22, 1865

Occupation - Foreman of Livery Stables - March 1, 1861

January 22, 1865

Superintendant Stables - December 21, 1862

- Joseph Garrett & Sarah Unknown

  o Joseph Garrett – bapt. 30 Jan 1738 (Baptism, **St. Nicholas Without Parish**)

Joseph Garrett (father):

Residence - Coombe - January 30, 1738

Hurst

- Joseph Garrett & Unknown

  ○ Sarah Martha Garrett & James E. Pim – 29 Sep 1880 (Marriage, **St. Stephen Parish**)

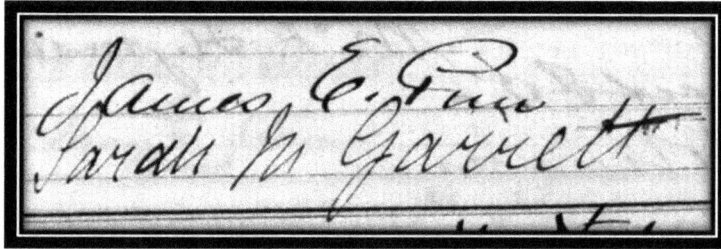

Signatures:

Sarah Martha Garrett (daughter):

   Residence - 60 Lower Mount Street - September 29, 1880

James E. Pim, son of Edward Pim (son-in-law):

   Residence - 65 Percy Place - September 29, 1880

   Occupation - Diamond Seller - September 29, 1880

Edward Pim (father):

   Occupation - Tailor

Joseph Garrett (father):

   Occupation - Manager in Sewell's Depository

Garrett Surname Ireland: 1600s to 1900s

Wedding Witnesses:

Thomas A. Lawrence & Emily Rogers

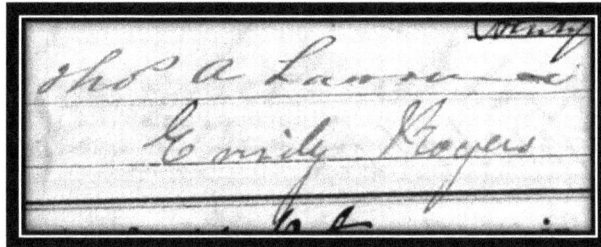

Signatures:

- Lawrence Garrett & Unknown

  o Richard Garrett – bapt. 2 Dec 1701 (Baptism, **St. Catherine Parish**)

- Martin Garrett & Catherine Ennis

  o Bridget Garrett – bapt. 25 Nov 1770 (Baptism, **St. Nicholas Parish (RC)**)

- Martin Garrett & Unknown

  o John Garrett – bapt. 13 Jun 1631 (Baptism, **St. John Parish**)

- Michael Garrett & Abigail Betagh

  o Mary Anne Garrett – bapt. 24 Jun 1801 (Baptism, **St. Michan Parish (RC)**)

- Michael Garrett & Elizabeth Reilly

  o Terence Garrett – b. 29 Apr 1861, bapt. 3 May 1861 (Baptism, **St. Mary, Pro Cathedral Parish (RC)**)

Michael Garrett (father):

Residence - 34 Lower Dominick Street - May 3, 1861

Hurst

- Michael Garrett & Ellen Hogarty

  o Patrick Garrett – bapt. 30 Jan 1828 (Baptism, Courcy's Country or Ballinspittal Parish (RC))

- Michael Garrett & Ellen Keefe

  o Michael Garrett – bapt. Jan 1824 (Baptism, Clontead Parish (RC))

- Michael Garrett & Honor Fitzgerald

  o Unknown Garrett – bapt. 1809 (Baptism, Clontead Parish (RC))

- Michael Garrett & Honor Murray

  o Ellen Garrett – bapt. Oct 1811 (Baptism, Clontead Parish (RC))

  o Joan Garrett – bapt. Dec 1812 (Baptism, Clontead Parish (RC))

- Michael Garrett & Honor Ryan

  o Ellen Garrett – bapt. 1822 (Baptism, Clontead Parish (RC))

- Michael Garrett & Joan Burke

  o Patrick Garrett – bapt. 24 Feb 1837 (Baptism, Rossalettiri & Kilkeraunmor (Roscarbery & Lissevard) Parish (RC))

- Michael Garrett & Margaret McCarthy

  o Ellen Garrett – bapt. 28 Feb 1838 (Baptism, Clontead Parish (RC))

  o Jane Garrett – bapt. 24 Aug 1840 (Baptism, Clontead Parish (RC))

- Michael Garrett & Mary Murphy

  o Patrick Garrett – bapt. 5 Mar 1820 (Baptism, Clontead Parish (RC))

- Michael Garrett & Mary Walters

  o Michael Garrett – bapt. 1 Feb 1817 (Baptism, SS. Michael & John Parish (RC))

Garrett Surname Ireland: 1600s to 1900s

- Michael Garrett & Mary Anne Garrett

  - Mary Garrett & Thomas Slator – 18 Sep 1871 (Marriage, **St. Mary, Pro Cathedral Parish (RC)**)

    - Catherine Slator – b. 4 Feb 1872, bapt. 3 Mar 1872 (Baptism, **Rathmines Parish** (RC))

    - Mary Anne Slator – b. 21 Jun 1873, bapt. 6 Jul 1873 (Baptism, **Rathmines Parish** (RC))

    - Catherine Slator – b. 1875, bapt. 1875 (Baptism, **St. Andrew Parish** (RC))

Mary Garrett (daughter):

Residence - 11 Langrish Place - September 18, 1871

Thomas Slator, son of Gulielmo Slator & Catherine Slator (son-in-law):

Residence - 11 Langrish Place - September 18, 1871

Wharton Terrace - March 3, 1872

July 6, 1873

43 Deuzille Street - 1875

Wedding Witnesses:

Gulielmo Kerwick & Margaret Slator

Hurst

- Michael Garrett & Unknown

  - John Garrett & Jane Young – 9 Jul 1855 (Marriage, **St. Michan Parish**)

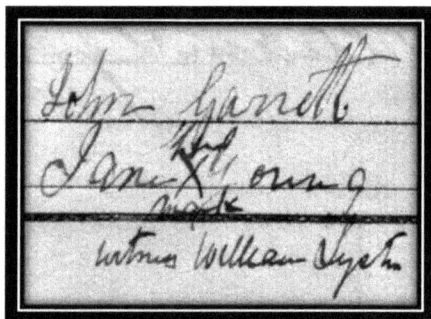

Signatures:

John Garrett (son):

 Residence - Kingstown - July 9, 1855

 Occupation - Policeman - July 9, 1855

Jane Young, daughter of Thomas Young (daughter-in-law):

 Residence - 3 Colerain Street - July 9, 1855

 Occupation - Dressmaker - July 9, 1855

Thomas Young (father):

 Occupation - Quarter Master, 59th Regiment

Michael Garrett (father):

 Occupation - Farmer

Wedding Witnesses:

John Leech & John Murphy

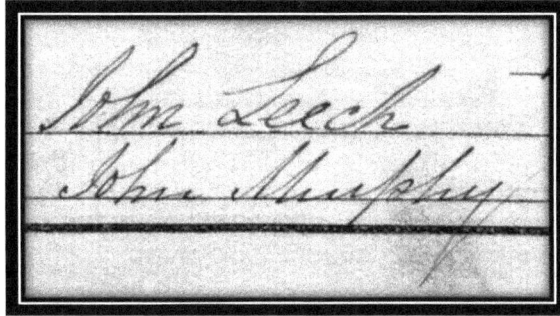

Signatures:

- Michael Garrett & Unknown

  o Alice Garrett & John Couch – 1 Aug 1876 (Marriage, **St. Peter Parish**)

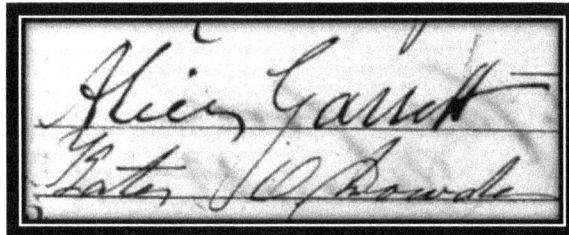

Signatures:

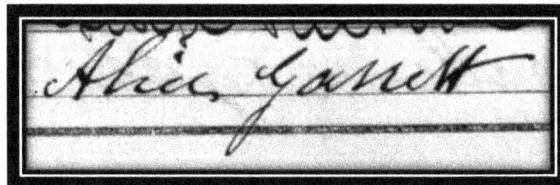

Signatures (Marriage):

Alice Garrett (daughter):

    Residence - 4 Wharton's Terrace - August 1, 1876

John Couch, son of John Couch (son-in-law):

    Residence - Portobello Barracks - August 1, 1876

    Occupation - Private, Army Service Corps - August 1, 1876

John Couch (father):

    Occupation - Laborer

Michael Garrett (father):

    Occupation - Soldier

Wedding Witnesses:

John Fletcher & Margaret Garrett

Signatures:

Garrett Surname Ireland: 1600s to 1900s

- Ned Garrett & Judy Murphy
  - Margaret Garrett – bapt. 15 Nov 1844 (Baptism, **Clontead Parish (RC)**)

- Ned Garrett & Margaret Keefe
  - Judy Garrett – bapt. 24 Jun 1838 (Baptism, **Clontead Parish (RC)**)
  - Mary Garrett – bapt. 9 Feb 1842 (Baptism, **Clontead Parish (RC)**)

- Patrick Garrett & Mary Unknown
  - Peter Garrett – bapt. 6 Jul 1747 (Baptism, **St. Catherine Parish (RC)**)

- Peter Garrett & Elizabeth Boylin – 8 Apr 1729 (Marriage, **St. Nicholas Within Parish**)

- Peter Garrett & Elizabeth Garrett
  - Catherine Garrett – bapt. 24 Dec 1749 (Baptism, **St. Luke Parish**)
  - Sarah Garrett – bapt. 28 Sep 1758 (Baptism, **St. Luke Parish**)

- Peter Garrett & Ellen Mullen – 19 Jun 1845 (Marriage, **St. Andrew Parish (RC)**)
  - Catherine Mary Garrett – bapt. 1846 (Baptism, **St. Andrew Parish (RC)**)

Wedding Witnesses:

James Mooney & Mary Anne Carberry

- Peter Garrett & Jane Garrett
  - James Garrett – bapt. 27 Jul 1787 (Baptism, **St. Paul Parish**)

- Peter Garrett & Mary Garrett
  - Margaret Garrett – bapt. 1764 (Baptism, **St. Andrew Parish (RC)**)
  - Sarah Garrett – b. 1766, bapt. 23 Nov 1766 (Baptism, **St. Catherine Parish (RC)**)
  - Sarah Garrett – b. 1767, bapt. 23 Jan 1767 (Baptism, **St. Catherine Parish (RC)**)
  - Thomas Garrett – bapt. 18 Sep 1772 (Baptism, **St. Mary, Pro Cathedral Parish (RC)**)

- Richard Garrett & Elizabeth Garrett

  - Jane Garrett – bapt. 20 Aug 1763 (Baptism, **St. Mary Parish**)

  - Thomas Garrett – bapt. 22 Feb 1767 (Baptism, **St. Mary Parish**)

  - John Garrett – bapt. 14 May 1769 (Baptism, **St. Mary Parish**)

Richard Garrett (father):

Residence - Sackville Lane - February 22, 1767

May 14, 1769

- Richard Garrett & Judith Garrett

  - Bridget Garrett – bapt. 4 Mar 1742 (Baptism, **St. Catherine Parish (RC)**)

- Richard Garrett & Unknown

  - Joseph Richard Garrett & Sarah Unknown

Signature:

- Elizabeth Lauder Garrett – b. 4 Dec 1857, bapt. 10 Feb 1858 (Baptism, **St. Catherine Parish**)

- Richard Garrett – b. 2 Jul 1859, bapt. 3 Aug 1859 (Baptism, **St. Catherine Parish**)

- Thomas Gregg Garrett – b. 17 Sep 1860, bapt. 28 Nov 1860 (Baptism, **St. Catherine Parish**)

- Isabel Alexander Garrett – b. 23 May 1863, bapt. 17 Jun 1863 (Baptism, **St. Catherine Parish**)

Garrett Surname Ireland: 1600s to 1900s

- William Lauder Garrett – b. 26 Sep 1864, bapt. 19 Oct 1864 (Baptism, **St. Catherine Parish**)

- Mary Cornelia (C o r n e l i a) Garrett – b. 15 May 1866, bapt. 6 Jun 1866 (Baptism, **St. Catherine Parish**)

Joseph Richard Garrett (son):

Residence - 1 Upper Parnell Place - February 10, 1858

August 3, 1859

November 28, 1860

June 17, 1863

October 19, 1864

June 6, 1866

Occupation - Gentleman - February 10, 1858

August 3, 1859

November 28, 1860

June 17, 1863

October 19, 1864

June 6, 1866

Hurst

○ Caroline Garrett & Thomas Huband Gregg – 28 Apr 1864 (Marriage, **St. Catherine Parish**)

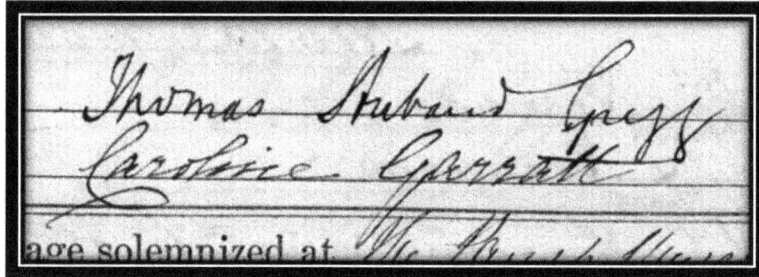

Signatures:

Caroline Garrett (daughter):

Residence - 1 Upper Parnell Place - April 28, 1864

Kilcommon Cahir - April 28, 1864

Thomas Huband Gregg, son of Francis T. Gregg (son-in-law):

Residence - Portland Weymouth - April 28, 1864

Occupation - Clerk in Holy Orders - April 28, 1864

Francis T. Gregg (father):

Occupation - Rector of Bally Macormick

Richard Garrett (father):

Occupation - Gentleman

Wedding Witnesses:

Joseph Richard Garrett & William Henry Gregg

Signatures:

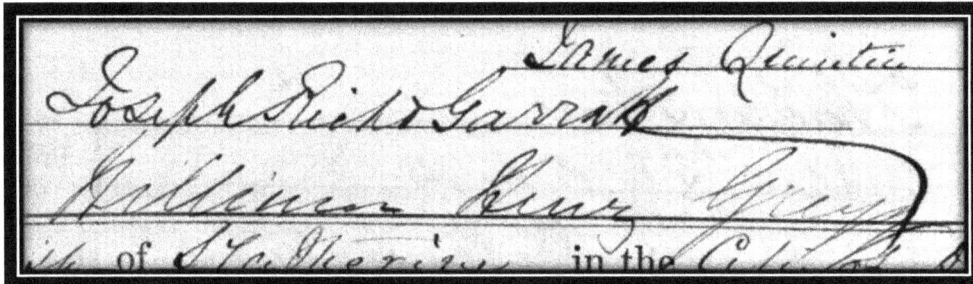

- Richard Garrett & Unknown

  - Elizabeth Jane Garrett (1st Marriage) & Unknown Sweeny

  - Elizabeth Jane Garrett Sweeny (2nd Marriage) & Arthur H. Reed – 9 Nov 1866 (Marriage, **St. Thomas Parish**)

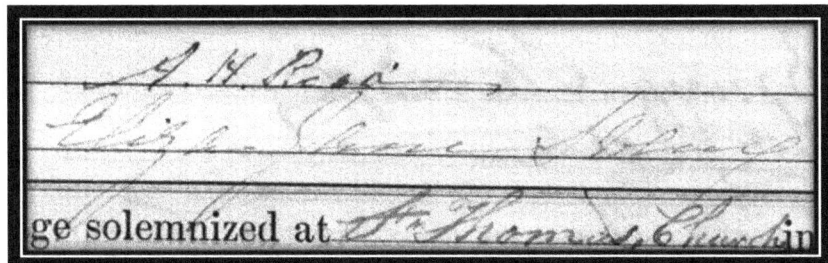

Signatures:

Elizabeth Jane Garrett Sweeny (daughter):

  Residence - Heath Ville, Monkstown, Co., Dublin - November 9, 1866

  Relationship Status at 2nd Marriage - widow

Hurst

Arthur H. Reed, son of John M. Reed (son-in-law):

    Residence - 15 Upper Sackville Street - November 9, 1866

    Occupation - Esquire - November 9, 1866

    Relationship Status at Marriage - widow

John M. Reed (father):

    Occupation - Esquire

Richard Garrett (father):

    Occupation - Esquire

Wedding Witnesses:

William A. Garrett & Henry Garrett

Signatures:

Garrett Surname Ireland: 1600s to 1900s

- Richard Garrett & Unknown

  - Elizabeth Galloway Garrett, b. 1867 & Edward White – 5 Apr 1887 (Marriage, **Leeson Park Parish**)

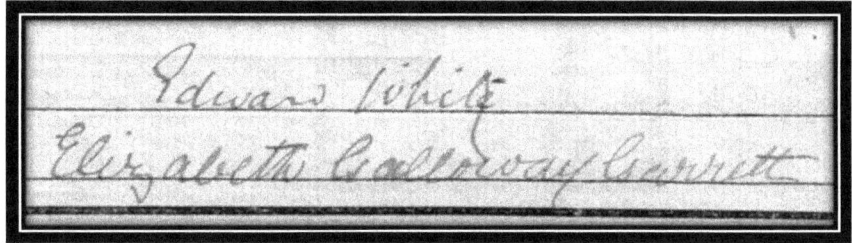

Signatures:

Elizabeth Galloway Garrett (daughter):

   Residence - Crawford Square, Londonderry - April 5, 1887

Edward White, son of Edward White (son-in-law):

   Residence - 114 Upper Leeson Street - April 5, 1887

   Occupation - Solicitor - April 5, 1887

Edward White (father):

   Occupation - Gentleman

Richard Garrett (father):

   Occupation - County Inspector R I C

Hurst

Wedding Witnesses:

R. Garrett & A. White

Signatures:

- Robert Garrett & Mary Garrett

  - William Garrett – bapt. 10 Jun 1734 (Baptism, **Kilnaughtin Parish**)

Robert Garrett (father):

Residence - Tarbert - June 10, 1734

- Robert Garrett & Mary Unknown

  - Robert Garrett – bapt. 11 Jan 1782 (Baptism, **St. Werburgh Parish**)

Robert Garrett (father):

Residence - Essex Street - January 11, 1782

Garrett Surname Ireland: 1600s to 1900s

- Robert Garrett & Unknown

  o Algernon (A l g e r n on) Robert Garrett & Elizabeth Harriet King – 16 Sep 1856 (Marriage, **St. Peter Parish**)

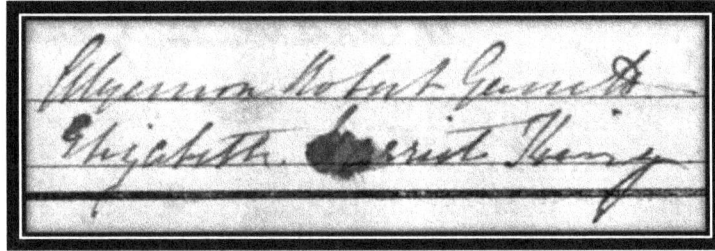

Signatures:

Algernon Robert Garrett (son):

　　Residence - Macken's Hotel, Dawson Street, St. Anne Parish -

　　　　　　　　　　　　　　　　　　　　September 16, 1856

　　Occupation - Brevet Major 46th Regiment - September 16, 1856

Elizabeth Harriet King, daughter of Charles King (daughter-in-law):

　　Residence - Mespil Villa - September 16, 1856

Charles King (father):

　　Occupation - Colonel in the Army

Robert Garrett (father):

　　Occupation - Major General

Hurst

Wedding Witnesses:

Augustus S. O. King & H. C. Hammel

Signatures:

- Robert Garrett & Unknown
  - James Garrett & Mary Moon – 19 Jan 1888 (Marriage, **St. Peter Parish**)

Signatures:

James Garrett (son):

Residence - Milltown Park, Shinrone, King's County - January 19, 1888

Occupation - Land Steward - January 19, 1888

Mary Moon, daughter of William Moon (daughter-in-law):

Residence - 21 York Street - January 19, 1888

Coolderrry House, Carrickmacross - January 19, 1888

William Moon (father):

Occupation - Land Steward

Garrett Surname Ireland: 1600s to 1900s

Robert Garrett (father):

Occupation - Land Agent

Wedding Witnesses:

Edward Rogers & Emily Rogers

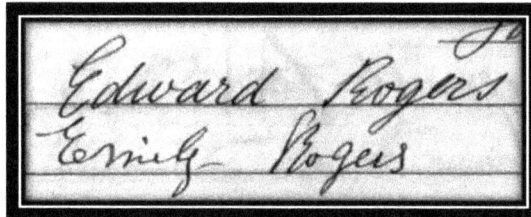

Signatures:

- Samuel Garrett & Catherine Unknown

  o Mary Garrett – bapt. 1841 (Baptism, **St. Andrew Parish** (RC))

- Samuel Garrett & Sarah Manning – 9 Jan 1803 (Marriage, **St. Paul Parish**)

- Samuel Garrett & Unknown

  o John Garrett & Elizabeth Kenish Joachins – 15 Jul 1869 (Marriage, **Kilmainham Parish**)

    ▪ Eleanor Garrett – b. 13 Apr 1862, bapt. 20 Apr 1862 (Baptism, **Kilmainham Parish**)

    ▪ Henry John Garrett – b. 30 May 1870, bapt. 3 Jul 1870 (Baptism, **Kilmainham Parish**)

John Garrett (son):

Residence - Inchicore - April 20, 1862

July 15, 1869

July 3, 1870

Hurst

Occupation - Engine Driver - April 20, 1862

July 15, 1869

July 3, 1870

Relationship Status at Marriage - widow

Elizabeth Kenish Joachins, daughter of William Kenish (daughter-in-law):

Residence - Inchicore - July 15, 1869

Relationship Status at Marriage - widow

William Kenish (father):

Occupation - Farmer

Samuel Garret (father):

Occupation - Contractor

Wedding Witnesses:

George Garrett & Martha Garrett

Signatures:

Garrett Surname Ireland: 1600s to 1900s

- Samuel Garrett & Unknown

  o Mercy Garrett & Robert Collier Burns (B u r n s) – 10 Jun 1875 (Marriage, **St. Peter Parish**)

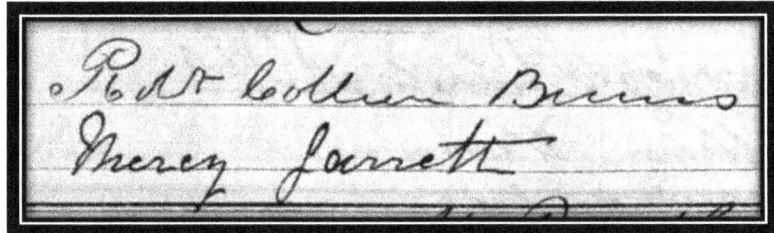

Signatures:

Mercy Garrett (daughter):

   Residence - 19 Fitzwilliam Square - June 10, 1875

Robert Collier Burns, son of William Burns (son-in-law):

   Residence - Ballina, Co., Mayo - June 10, 1875

   Occupation - Cabinet Maker - June 10, 1875

   Relationship Status at Marriage - widow

William Burns (father):

   Occupation - Shopkeeper

Samuel Garrett (father):

   Occupation - Stone Merchant

Hurst

Wedding Witnesses:

John Maurice McCullough & Emma Warland

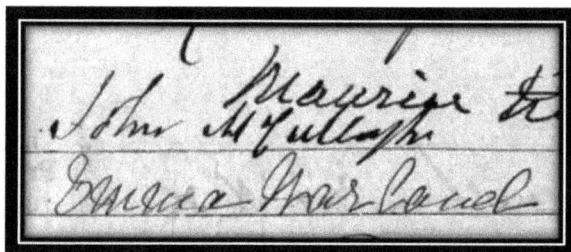

Signatures:

- Thomas Garrett & Ada Bryan Garrett

  ○ Frances Emma Garrett – b. 18 Oct 1854, bapt. 1 Jan 1858 (Baptism, **St. Mark Parish**)

  ○ Blanche Garrett – b. 4 Nov 1857, bapt. 1 Jan 1858 (Baptism, **St. Mark Parish**)

Thomas Garrett (father):

Residence - 15 Queen Square - January 1, 1858

Occupation - Accountant - January 1, 1858

- Thomas Garrett & Anne Unknown

  ○ James Garrett – bapt. 9 Jun 1790 (Baptism, **St. Audoen Parish (RC)**)

- Thomas Garrett & Dorcas Gorman (G o r m a n) – 7 Aug 1795 (Marriage, **Cork - SS. Peter & Paul Parish (RC)**)

  ○ Mary Garrett – bapt. 5 Sep 1798 (Baptism, **Cork - SS. Peter & Paul Parish (RC)**)

Thomas Garrett (father):

Residence - Harper's Lane - September 5, 1798

Garrett Surname Ireland: 1600s to 1900s

Dorcas Gorman (mother):

Residence - Old Bridewell Lane - August 7, 1795

Wedding Witnesses:

John Sullivan, William Sullivan, & Anne Garrett

- Thomas Garrett & Elizabeth Garrett

  o Rachel Garrett – bapt. 21 Jul 1763 (Baptism, **Aghold Parish**)

- Thomas Garrett & Ellen Haley – 8 Jan 1844 (Marriage, **Cork - South Parish** (RC))

  o Ellen Mary Garrett – bapt. 8 Feb 1843 (Baptism, **Cork - South Parish** (RC))

- Thomas Garrett & Honor Garrett

  o John Garrett – bapt. 28 Aug Unclear (Baptism, **Aghold Parish**)

- Thomas Garrett & Jane Unknown

  o Charles Garrett – bapt. 17 May 1812 (Baptism, **St. John Parish**)

Thomas Garrett (father):

Occupation - Nottingham Militia - May 17, 1812

- Thomas Garrett & Margaret Unknown

  o Thomas Garrett – bapt. 7 Feb 1757 (Baptism, **St. Michan Parish** (RC))

- Thomas Garrett & Mary Garrett

  o Lydia Garrett – bapt. 13 Dec 1772 (Baptism, **St. Luke Parish**)

Thomas Garrett (father):

Residence - Truck Street - December 13, 1772

Occupation - Worsted Weaver - December 13, 1772

Hurst

- Thomas Garrett & Mary Unknown

  - Unknown Garrett – bapt. Sep 1724 (Baptism, **St. John Parish**)

  - Jane Garrett – bapt. May 1726 (Baptism, **St. John Parish**)

Thomas Garrett (father):

Residence - Essex Street - September 1724

May 1726

Occupation - Glover - September 1724

May 1726

- Thomas Garrett & Mary Unknown

  - Thomas Garrett – bapt. 13 Aug 1775 (Baptism, **St. Catherine Parish**)

Thomas Garrett (father):

Residence - Coombe - August 13, 1775

- Thomas Garrett & Unknown

Signature:

  - Sarah Garrett & Thomas L'Estrange – 8 Jun 1850 (Marriage, **St. George Parish**)

Signatures:

Sarah Garrett (daughter):

Residence - 17 North Frederick Street - June 8, 1850

Thomas L'Estrange, son of Torriano Francis L'Estrange (son-in-law):

Residence - Kilnagama, Kings County - June 8, 1850

Occupation - Solicitor - June 8, 1850

Torriano Francis L'Estrange (father):

Occupation - Lieutenant in the Army

Thomas Garrett (father):

Occupation - Solicitor

Wedding Witnesses:

Thomas Garrett & Thomas Mulock

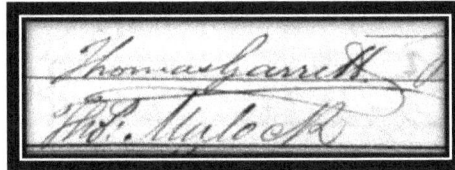

Signatures:

- Timothy Garrett & Margaret Keohane
  - Cornelius (C o r n e l i u s) Garrett – bapt. 30 May 1809 (Baptism, **Bantry Parish** (RC))
- Unknown Garrett & Catherine Unknown
  - Joseph Garrett – b. 1896, bapt. 1896 (Baptism, **St. Andrew Parish** (RC))

Unknown Garrett (father):

Residence - Holles Street Hospital - 1896

Hurst

- Unknown Garrett & Mary Unknown

  - Unknown Garrett – bapt. May 1752 (Baptism, **St. James Parish**)

- Unknown Garrett & Unknown

  - Edward Garrett

Signature:

- Unknown Garrett & Unknown

  - Elizabeth Garrett

Signature:

- Unknown Garrett & Unknown

  - Ellen Garrett

Signature:

- Unknown Garrett & Unknown

  o George Garrett

Signature:

- Unknown Garrett & Unknown

  o Harriet Garrett

Signature:

- Unknown Garrett & Unknown

  o Henry Garrett

Signature:

- Unknown Garrett & Unknown

  o Martin Garrett

Signature:

- Unknown Garrett & Unknown

  o R. C. Garrett

Signatures:

- Unknown Garrett & Unknown

  o William Alexander Garrett

Signature:

- William Garrett & Barbara Wilson, bur. 17 Aug 1707 (Burial, **St. John Parish**) – 22 Jun 1668

  (Marriage, **St. Michael Parish**)

  o Samuel Garrett – bapt. 21 Dec 1680 (Baptism, **St. John Parish**)

- William Garrett & Deborah Nolan

  o Mary Jane Garrett – b. 24 Aug 1885, bapt. 31 Aug 1885 (Baptism, **St. Michan Parish (RC)**)

William Garrett (father):

Residence - 9 Anne Street - August 31, 1885

Garrett Surname Ireland: 1600s to 1900s

- William Garrett & Elizabeth Unknown

  o James Garrett – bapt. 2 Apr 1753 (Baptism, **St. John Parish**)

- William Garrett & Ellen Dennis

  o William Abraham Garrett – b. 10 Aug 1851, bapt. 16 Nov 1851 (Baptism, **St. Mary Parish**)

  o Ellen Garrett, b. 24 Jun 1853, bapt. 4 Jul 1855 (Baptism, **St. Mary Parish**) & John Mann –

    19 Apr 1871 (Marriage, **St. Michan Parish**)

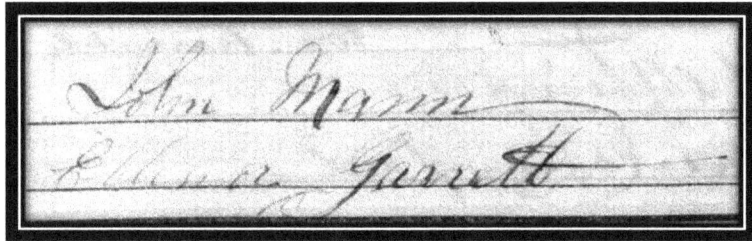

Signatures:

Ellen Garrett (daughter):

    Residence - 2 Lurgan Street - April 19, 1871

    Relationship Status at Marriage - under age

John Mann, son of William Mann (son-in-law):

    Residence - Linen Hall Barracks - April 19, 1871

    Occupation - Sergeant of 27th Regiment - April 19, 1871

William Mann (father):

    Occupation - Sergeant Major, Staff

William Garrett (father):

    Occupation - Commission Agent

Hurst

Wedding Witnesses:

Joseph Windrum & Ellen McGowan

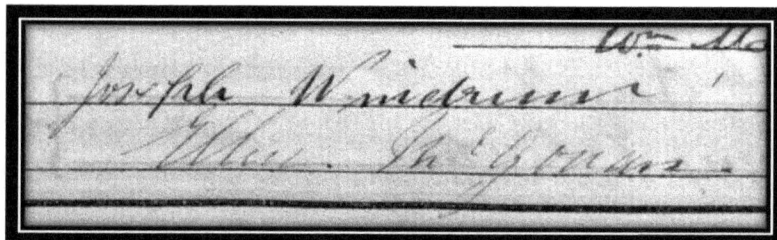

Signatures:

- Isabel Garrett – b. 6 May 1855, bapt. 4 Jul 1855 (Baptism, **St. Mary Parish**)

- Mary Teresa Garrett – b. 6 May 1855, bapt. 22 Jun 1855 (Baptism, **St. Michan Parish** (RC))

- Martha Garrett – b. 4 Jun 1859, bapt. 22 Jun 1859 (Baptism, **St. Michan Parish** (RC))

- Martha Alice Garrett – b. 12 Jun 1859, bapt. 17 Jul 1859 (Baptism, **St. Mary Parish**)

- Isaac Garrett – b. 16 Feb 1861, bapt. 22 Apr 1861 (Baptism, **St. Michan Parish** (RC))

- Edward William Garrett – b. 10 Jul 1864, bapt. 20 Jul 1864 (Baptism, **St. Michan Parish** (RC))

- Edward Garrett Garrett – b. 11 Jul 1864, bapt. 22 Sep 1876 (Baptism, **St. Mary Parish**)

William Garrett (father):

Residence - 2 Lurgan Street - November 16, 1851

June 22, 1855

July 4, 1855

June 22, 1859

July 17, 1859

April 22, 1861

Garrett Surname Ireland: 1600s to 1900s

July 20, 1864

September 22, 1876

Occupation - Salesman - November 16, 1851

July 17, 1859

Clerk - July 4, 1855

Commission Agent - September 22, 1876

- William Garrett & Judith Unknown

  o Mary Garrett – bapt. 9 Aug 1746 (Baptism, **St. Michan Parish** (RC))

  o William Garrett – bapt. 28 Oct 1748 (Baptism, **St. Michan Parish** (RC))

  o Margaret Garrett – bapt. 26 Dec 1750 (Baptism, **St. Michan Parish** (RC))

  o Bartholomew Garrett – bapt. 25 Aug 1752 (Baptism, **St. Michan Parish** (RC))

  o Jane Garrett – bapt. 6 Jul 1755 (Baptism, **St. Michan Parish** (RC))

  o Jane Garrett – bapt. 6 Jul 1757 (Baptism, **St. Michan Parish** (RC))

  o Elizabeth Garrett – bapt. 28 Jun 1759 (Baptism, **St. Michan Parish** (RC))

- William Garrett & Mary Unknown

  o Mary Anne Garrett – b. 20 May 1835, bapt. 28 Jun 1835 (Baptism, **St. Peter Parish**)

William Garrett (father):

Residence - 22 Chancery Lane, St. Bridget Parish - June 28, 1835

Hurst

- William Garrett & Unknown

  - Catherine Garrett & William Lace – 17 Oct 1853 (Marriage, **St. Peter Parish**)

Signatures:

Catherine Garrett (daughter):

   Residence - 13 Holles Street - October 17, 1853

William Lace, son of Philip Lace (son-in-law):

   Residence - 6 Holles Row - October 17, 1853

   Occupation - Harness Maker - October 17, 1853

Philip Lace (father):

   Occupation - Farmer

William Garrett (father):

   Occupation - Miller

Wedding Witnesses:

Thomas Wilson & Margaret Walsh

Signatures:

- William Garrett & Unknown
  - ○ Edward Garrett & Elizabeth Field – 24 Mar 1869 (Marriage, **St. George Parish**)

Signatures:

Edward Garrett (son):

Residence - 5 Summer Street - March 24, 1869

Occupation - Brass Founder - March 24, 1869

Elizabeth Field, daughter of Richard Field (daughter-in-law):

Residence - 5 Summer Street - March 24, 1869

Richard Field (father):

Occupation - Boot Maker

Hurst

William Garrett (father):

  Occupation - Brass Founder

Wedding Witnesses:

William Henry Harding & Sarah Duncan

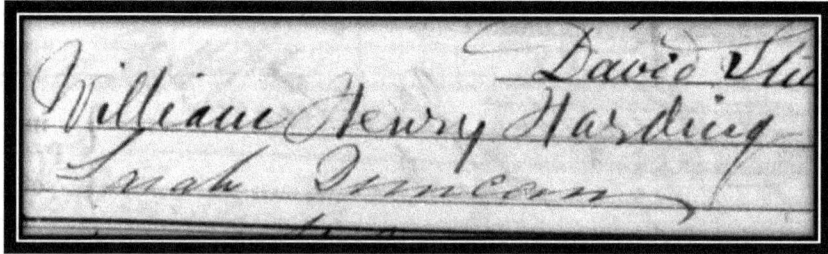

Signatures:

- William Alexander Garrett & Arabella Garrett
    - Georgina Caroline Garrett – b. 28 Apr 1864, bapt. 24 Aug 1864 (Baptism, **St. Luke Parish**)
    - Charlotte Amelia Garrett – b. 1 Dec 1865, bapt. 31 Aug 1866 (Baptism, **St. Luke Parish**)

William Alexander Garrett (father):

  Residence - 1 Kenilworth Square - August 24, 1864

    Peare Mount, Rathgar Road - August 31, 1866

  Occupation - Cashier in Majors Lotouche's Bank - August 24, 1864

                                August 31, 1866

Garrett Surname Ireland: 1600s to 1900s

- William Alexander Garrett & Mary Louisa Garrett

  o Florence Maude Garrett – b. 11 Dec 1875, bapt. 14 Jan 1876 (Baptism, **Rathmines Parish**)

William Alexander Garrett (father):

Residence - 3 Leinster Road - January 14, 1876

Occupation - Captain in Tips Light Infantry - January 14, 1876

Individual Baptisms/Births

- Benjamin Garrett – bapt. 28 Jul 1731 (Baptism, **St. Paul Parish**)

- Henry Garrett – bapt. 16 Aug 1826 (Baptism, **Urglin Parish**)

Henry Garrett (child):

Residence - Grangeford Parish - August 16, 1826

- John Garrett – bapt. 4 Dec 1743 (Baptism, **St. Paul Parish**)

- Peter Paul Garrett – b. 1878, bapt. 1878 (Baptism, **Chapelizod Parish** (RC))

Peter Paul Garrett (child):

Residence - Chapelizod - 1878

- Thomas Garrett – bapt. 11 Dec 1743 (Baptism, **St. Paul Parish**)

Individual Burials

- Alice Garrett – b. 1800, bur. 28 Feb 1834 (Burial, **St. Paul Parish**)

Alice Garrett (deceased):

> Age at Death - 34 years

- Alice Garrett – b. 1855, bur. 20 May 1858 (Burial, **St. Luke Parish**)

Alice Garrett (deceased):

> Residence - Cork Street - before May 20, 1858

> Age at Death - 3 years

- Anne Garret – b. 1670, bur. 27 Apr 1726 (Burial, **St. Werburgh Parish**)

Anne Garrett (deceased):

> Residence - Gun Alley - before April 27, 1726

> Age at Death - 56 years

> Cause of Death - fever

- Anne Garrett – bur. 7 Apr 1783 (Burial, **St. James Parish**)

Anne Garrett (deceased):

> Residence - Boot Lane - before April 7, 1783

Hurst

- Anne Garrett – bur. 21 May 1798 (Burial, **St. Nicholas Without Parish**)

Anne Garrett (deceased):

Residence - Coombe - before May 21, 1798

- Bridget Garrett – bur. 13 Nov 1763 (Burial, **St. James Parish**)

Bridget Garrett (deceased):

Residence - Thomas Court - before November 13, 1763

- Catherine Garrett – bur. 23 Aug 1669 (Burial, **St. Peter Parish**)
- Catherine Garrett – bur. 1 Mar 1744 (Burial, **St. James Parish**)

Catherine Garrett (deceased):

Residence - Copper Alley - before March 1, 1744

- Daniel Garrett – bur. 30 Jul 1740 (Burial, **St. Audoen Parish**)

Daniel Garrett (deceased):

Residence - Market - before July 30, 1740

- David Garrett – bur. 21 May 1796 (Burial, **St. Catherine Parish**)

David Garrett (deceased):

Residence - Thomas Street - before May 21, 1796

Garrett Surname Ireland: 1600s to 1900s

- David Garrett – bur. 21 May 1797 (Burial, **St. Catherine Parish**)

- David Garrett – d. 7 Dec 1867, bur. 1867 (Burial, **St. James Parish**)

David Garrett (deceased):

Residence - South Dublin Union - December 7, 1867

- Edward Garrett – b. 1728, d. 16 Nov 1788 (Burial, **St. Anne Parish**)

Edward Garrett (deceased):

Age at Death - 60 years

- Eleanor Garrett – bur. 12 Nov 1726 (Burial, **St. Mary Parish**)

- Eleanor Garrett – bur. 28 Jan 1728 (Burial, **St. John Parish**)

Eleanor Garrett (deceased):

Residence - St. James - before January 28, 1728

- Elizabeth Garrett – bur. 14 Aug 1768 (Burial, **St. Audoen Parish**)

- Elizabeth Garrett – bur. 24 Dec 1799 (Burial, **St. Nicholas Without Parish**)

Elizabeth Garrett (deceased):

Residence - Thomas Street - before December 24, 1799

- Frances Garrett – bur. 4 Dec 1806 (Burial, **St. Nicholas Without Parish**)

Frances Garrett (deceased):

Residence - Grand Walk - before December 4, 1806

- Francis Garrett – bur. 28 Dec 1790 (Burial, **St. Paul Parish**)

Hurst

- George Garrett – b. 1822, bur. 26 May 1823 (Burial, **St. Nicholas Without Parish**)

George Garrett (deceased):

  Residence - Bishop Street - before May 26, 1823

  Age at Death - 1 year

- George Garrett – bur. 26 May 1824 (Burial, **St. Nicholas Without Parish**)

George Garrett (deceased):

  Residence - Bishop Street - before May 26, 1824

- George Garrett – b. 1830, bur. 20 Aug 1890 (Burial, **St. George Parish**)

George Garrett (deceased):

  Residence - James Street - before August 20, 1890

  Age at Death - 60 years

- Henry Garrett – bur. 1 Dec 1713 (Burial, **St. Audoen Parish**)
- Henry Garrett – b. 1813, bur. 11 Jun 1838 (Burial, **Carlow Parish**)

Henry Garrett (deceased):

  Residence - Carlow - before June 11, 1838

  Age at Death - 25 years

  Professional Title - Reverend

- Hugh Garrett – bur. 14 Sep 1784 (Burial, **St. Paul Parish**)
- Hugh Garrett – bur. 23 Jun 1800 (Burial, **St. Paul Parish**)

Garrett Surname Ireland: 1600s to 1900s

- Humphrey Garrett – bur. 10 Feb 1794 (Burial, **St. Catherine Parish**)

- James Garrett – bur. 24 Jun 1671 (Burial, **St. Michan Parish**)

James Garrett (deceased):

Occupation - Butcher - before June 24, 1671

- James Garrett – bur. 1775 (Burial, **St. Paul Parish**)

- James Garrett – b. 1864, bur. 28 Jan 1879 (Burial, **St. George Parish**)

James Garrett (deceased):

Residence - 2 Kennedy's Lane - before January 28, 1879

Age at Death - 15 years

- Jane Garrett – bur. 22 Mar 1825 (Burial, **Glasnevin Parish**)

Jane Garrett (deceased):

Residence - Glasnevin - before March 22, 1825

- John Garrett – bur. 13 Nov 1683 (Burial, **St. Catherine Parish**)

- John Garrett – bur. 27 May 1715 (Burial, **St. Peter Parish**)

John Garrett (deceased):

Residence - King Street - before May 27, 1715

- John Garrett – bur. 11 Sep 1719 (Burial, **St. Nicholas Without Parish**)

John Garrett (deceased):

Residence - Francis Street - before September 11, 1719

Hurst

- John Garrett – bur. 3 Jun 1725 (Burial, **St. Catherine Parish**)

John Garrett (deceased):

    Remarks about Death - child

- John Garrett – bur. 29 Aug 1740 (Burial, **St. Paul Parish**)

- John Garrett – bur. 26 May 1748 (Burial, **St. Nicholas Within Parish**)

- John Garrett – bur. 26 May 1748 (Burial, **St. Nicholas Without Parish**)

- John Garrett – b. Mar 1833, bur. 13 May 1833 (Burial, **St. John Parish**)

John Garrett (deceased):

    Residence - Wood Quay - before May 13, 1833

    Age at Death - 3 months

- John Woods Garrett – b. Mar 1854, bur. 9 May 1854 (Burial, **St. George Parish**)

John Woods Garrett (deceased):

    Residence - Great Britain Street - before May 9, 1854

    Age at Death - 3 months

- Joseph Garrett – bur. 17 Apr 1738 (Burial, **St. Audoen Parish**)

Joseph Garrett (deceased):

    Residence - Channel Lane - before April 17, 1738

- Joseph Garrett – bur. 14 Jun 1804 (Burial, **St. Paul Parish**)

Garrett Surname Ireland: 1600s to 1900s

- Mary Garrett – bur. 21 Jun 1700 (Burial, **St. Nicholas Without Parish**)

Mary Garrett (deceased):

Residence - Upper Coombe - June 21, 1700

- Mary Garrett – bur. 29 Jun 1718 (Burial, **St. Nicholas Without Parish**)

Mary Garrett (deceased):

Residence - Francis Street - before June 29, 1718

- Mary Garrett – bur. 12 Jun 1722 (Burial, **St. Audoen Parish**)
- Mary Garrett – bur. 20 Nov 1740 (Burial, **St. Paul Parish**)
- Mary Garrett – bur. 9 Mar 1772 (Burial, **St. Peter Parish**)
- Mary Garrett – b. Dec 1848, d. 30 Aug 1849, bur. 31 Aug 1849 (Burial, **Arbour Hill Barracks Parish**)

Mary Garrett (deceased):

Age at Death - 9 months

Cause of Death - inflammation

Remarks about Death - Mary Garrett's father was in the 2nd Regiment.

- Mary Anne Garrett – bur. 24 Mar 1832 (Burial, **St. Paul Parish**)
- Michael Garrett – b. 1831, bur. 7 Sep 1831 (Burial, **St. George Parish**)

Michael Garrett (deceased):

Residence - Dorset Street - before September 7, 1831

Age at Death - 9 Weeks

Hurst

- Nicholas Garrett – bur. 13 Jun 1703 (Burial, **St. Peter Parish**)

Nicholas Garrett (deceased):

Residence - KE [Possibly King] **Street - before June 13, 1703**

- Peter Garrett – bur. 16 Jan 1710 (Burial, **St. Nicholas Without Parish**)

Peter Garrett (deceased):

Residence - Francis **Street - before January 16, 1710**

- Robert Garrett – bur. 28 Feb 1797 (Burial, **St. Catherine Parish**)

Robert Garrett (deceased):

Residence - Thomas **Street - before February 28, 1797**

- Samuel Garrett – bur. 25 Sep 1736 (Burial, **St. Luke Parish**)
- Sarah Garrett – bur. 26 Dec 1730 (Burial, **St. Catherine Parish**)
- Sarah Garrett – bur. 4 Dec 1748 (Burial, **St. James Parish**)

Sarah Garrett (deceased):

Residence - Fishamble **Street - before December 4, 1748**

- Sarah Garrett – bur. 28 Oct 1784 (Burial, **St. Luke Parish**)

Sarah Garrett (deceased):

Residence - Grafton **Street - before October 28, 1784**

Cause of Death - old age

Garrett Surname Ireland: 1600s to 1900s

- Sarah Garrett – b. 1831, bur. 1 Apr 1831 (Burial, **St. George Parish**)

Sarah Garrett (deceased):

    Residence - Nerney's Court - before April 1, 1831

    Age at Death - 5 weeks

- Susan Garrett – bur. 23 Oct 1736 (Burial, **St. Nicholas Without Parish**)

Susan Garrett (deceased):

    Residence - Francis Street - before October 23, 1736

- Susan Garrett – b. 1836, bur. 2 Jul 1877 (Burial, **St. George Parish**)

Susan Garrett (deceased):

    Residence - 16 Christ Church Place - before July 2, 1877

    Age at Death - 41 years

- Thomas Garrett – bur. Mar 1732 (Burial, **St. Audoen Parish**)

Thomas Garrett (deceased):

    Residence - Page's Alley - before March 1732

- Thomas Garrett – bur. 12 May 1789 (Burial, **St. Paul Parish**)

- Unknown Garrett – bur. 8 Mar 1713 (Burial, **St. Nicholas Without Parish**)

- Unknown Garrett – bur. 26 Apr 1730 (Burial, **St. John Parish**)

Hurst

- Unknown Garrett – bur. 17 Apr 1736 (Burial, **St. Nicholas Without Parish**)

Unknown Garrett (deceased):

    Residence - St. Andrew Parish - before April 17, 1736

- Unknown Garrett – bur. 14 Jan 1771 (Burial, **St. Nicholas Without Parish**)

Unknown Garrett (deceased):

    Residence - Steven Street - before January 14, 1771

- Unknown Garrett (Mr.) – bur. 6 Jan 1783 (Burial, **St. Mary Parish**)

Unknown Garrett (Mr.) (deceased):

    Residence - Liffey Street - before January 6, 1783

- Unknown Garrett (Mrs.) – bur. 2 Feb 1780 (Burial, **St. Mary Parish**)

Unknown Garrett (Mrs.) (deceased):

    Residence - Cole's Lane - before February 2, 1780

- William Garrett – bur. 26 Aug 1705 (Burial, **St. Catherine Parish**)
- William Garrett – bur. Aug 1715 (Burial, **St. Nicholas Without Parish**)

William Garrett (deceased):

    Residence - Jordan's Alley - before August 1715

- William Garrett – bur. 18 May 1794 (Burial, **St. John Parish**)

Individual Marriages

- Alice Garrett & Thomas Malone – 14 Aug 1820 (Marriage, **St. Andrew Parish (RC)**)

Wedding Witnesses:

Gulielmo Coughlin & Mary Grier

- Alice Anne Garrett & Augustus William Barry – 29 Dec 1836 (Marriage, **St. Mary Parish**)

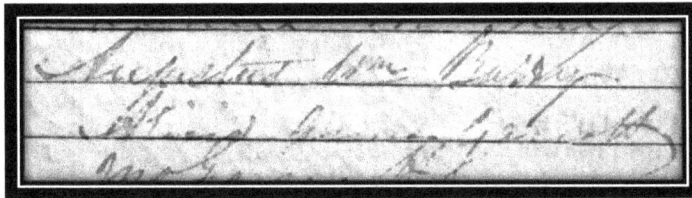

Signatures:

Alice Anne Garrett (wife):

　　Residence - St. George Parish - December 29, 1836

Augustus William Barry (husband):

　　Residence -St. Mary Parish - December 29, 1836

Wedding Witnesses:

John Garrett & Richard Jones

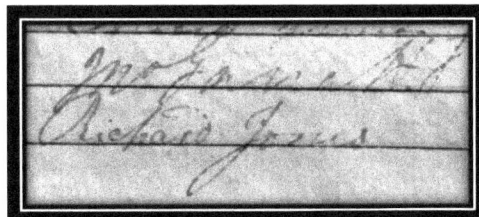

Signatures:

Hurst

- Anne Garrett & James Byrne (B y r n e)

  - James Byrne (B y r n e) – b. 29 Aug 1877, bapt. 30 Aug 1877 (Baptism, **SS. Michael & John Parish (RC)**)

  - Margaret Mary Byrne (B y r n e) – b. 29 Aug 1877, bapt. 30 Aug 1877 (Baptism, **SS. Michael & John Parish (RC)**)

  - Edward Byrne (B y r n e) – b. 23 Feb 1880, bapt. 27 Feb 1880 (Baptism, **St. Mary, Pro Cathedral Parish (RC)**)

  - Anne Byrne (B y r n e) – b. 27 Sep 1881, bapt. 3 Oct 1881 (Baptism, **St. Mary, Pro Cathedral Parish (RC)**)

James Byrne (father):

Residence - 2 George's Place - August 30, 1877

34 East Arran Street - February 27, 1880

154 Great Britain Street - October 3, 1881

- Anne Garrett & John Aagan

  - John Aagan – b. 20 Jul 1873, bapt. 25 Jul 1873 (Baptism, **St. Nicholas Parish (RC)**)

John Aagan (father):

Residence - 1 Brabazon Row - July 25, 1873

- Anne Garrett & Lawrence Sullivan – 13 Sep 1835 (Marriage, **Kinsale Parish (RC)**)

- Anne Garrett & Martin Molloy

  - Hugh Molloy – bapt. 9 May 1814 (Baptism, **SS. Michael & John Parish (RC)**)

- Anne Garrett & Richard Harris – 13 May 1844 (Marriage, **St. George Parish**)

Signatures:

Anne Garrett (wife):

Residence - 10 Upper Gardiner Street, St. George Parish - May 13, 1844

Richard Harris (husband):

Residence - 67 Harcourt Street, St. Peter Parish, Dublin - May 13, 1844

Occupation - Esquire - May 13, 1844

Wedding Witnesses:

George Garrett & William Faussett

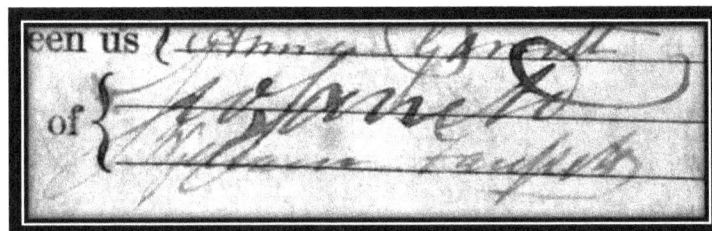

Signatures:

- Anne Garrett & William Creed

  - Roseanne Creed – bapt. 1864 (Baptism, **St. Mary Parish** (RC))

  - Christine Creed – b. 1872, bapt. 1872 (Baptism, **St. Mary Parish** (RC))

  - Thomas Creed – b. 1875, bapt. 1875 (Baptism, **St. Mary Parish** (RC))

Hurst

- Bridget Garrett & Jeremiah Ryan

  - Jeremiah Ryan & Mary Anne Grace – 1 Jun 1904 (Marriage, **St. Mary, Pro Cathedral Parish (RC)**)

Jeremiah Ryan (son):

Residence - 44 North King Street - June 1, 1904

Mary Anne Grace, daughter of Richard Grace & Ellen Handrahan

(daughter-in-law):

Residence - 60 Talbot Street - June 1, 1904

Wedding Witnesses:

Lawrence Ryan & Anne Kenny

- Catherine Garrett & Daniel Farley

  - John Farley – bapt. 4 Jun 1855 (Baptism, **Kinsale Parish (RC)**)

  - Mary Farley – bapt. 3 Oct 1858 (Baptism, **Kinsale Parish (RC)**)

- Catherine Garrett & John Daly

  - Mary Daly – bapt. 5 Mar 1837 (Baptism, **Kinsale Parish (RC)**)

John Daly (father):

Residence - Knockduff - March 5, 1837

- Catherine Garrett & Luke Whitaker – 5 Aug 1816 (Marriage, **Carlow Parish**)

- Catherine Garrett & Matthew Cook

  - Martha Agnes Cook – b. 1874, bapt. 1874 (Baptism, **St. Andrew Parish (RC)**)

Garrett Surname Ireland: 1600s to 1900s

Matthew Cook (father):

Residence - 1 Grattan Court - 1874

- Catherine Garrett & Michael Leahy

  o   Mary Leahy – bapt. Jan 1814 (Baptism, **Clontead Parish** (RC))

- Catherine Garrett & Richard Ball

  o   Richard Ball – bapt. 19 May 1817 (Baptism, **St. Michan Parish** (RC))

- Catherine Garrett & Timothy Cavanagh

  o   Julianne Cavanagh – bapt. 27 Sep 1796 (Baptism, **Bandon Parish** (RC))

- Catherine Garrett & William Alexander – Apr 1718 (Marriage, **St. Luke Parish**)

Catherine Garrett (wife):

Residence - St. Luke Parish - April 1718

- Catherine Garrett & William Shea

  o   Richard Shea – bapt. 16 Aug 1814 (Baptism, **Clontead Parish** (RC))

- Catherine Garrett & William Spain

  o   Michael Spain – bapt. Sep 1812 (Baptism, **Clontead Parish** (RC))

- Eleanor Garrett & William Clifford – 29 Jun 1760 (Marriage, **St. Michan Parish** (RC))

Wedding Witnesses:

Matthew Clifford, Eleanor Clifford, Elizabeth Beaghan, & Rose Farrell

- Elizabeth Garrett & Cornelius (C o r n e l i u s) Meagher – 16 Oct 1853 (Marriage, **St. Andrew Parish** (RC))

Hurst

Wedding Witnesses:

James Byrne & Anne Byrne

- Elizabeth Garrett & James Byrne (B y r n e)
  - Elizabeth Byrne (B y r n e) & Charles Traynor – 12 Apr 1868 (Marriage, **Rathmines Parish** (RC))

Elizabeth Byrne (daughter):

Residence - Synge Street - April 12, 1868

Charles Traynor, son of Michael Traynor & Mary Anne Kelly (son-in-law):

Residence - SS. Michael & John Parish - April 12, 1868

Wedding Witnesses:

James Garrett & Mary Anne Byrne

  - Mary Anne Byrne (B y r n e) & James Gaynor – 24 Jul 1883 (Marriage, **Harrington Street Parish** (RC))

Mary Anne Byrne (daughter):

Residence - 32 Synge Street - July 24, 1883

James Gaynor, son of Lewis Gaynor & Margaret Grennon (son-in-law):

Residence - 32 Synge Street - July 24, 1883

Wedding Witnesses:

Michael Timmons & Joan Rathgar

Garrett Surname Ireland: 1600s to 1900s

- Elizabeth Garrett & John Harlin

  o Mary Harlin – bapt. 5 Aug 1803 (Baptism, **SS. Michael & John Parish (RC)**)

  o James Harlin – bapt. 3 Aug 1804 (Baptism, **SS. Michael & John Parish (RC)**)

- Elizabeth Garrett & John Legrue

  o Margaret Legrue – b. 1874, bapt. 1874 (Baptism, **St. Andrew Parish (RC)**)

John Legrue (father):

Residence - 14 Wicklow Street - 1874

- Elizabeth Garrett & John Wilson – 28 Jul 1828 (Marriage, **St. George Parish**)

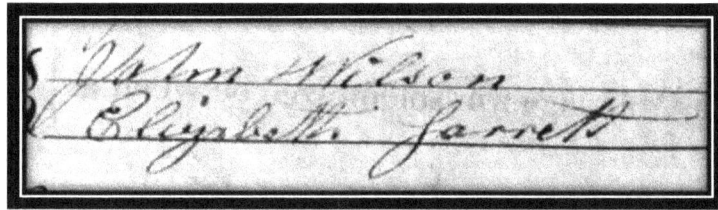

Signatures:

Elizabeth Garrett (wife):

Residence - St. Mary Parish - July 28, 1828

Relationship Status at Marriage - widow

John Wilson (husband):

Residence - St. George Parish - July 28, 1828

Hurst

Wedding Witnesses:

Thomas Woods & James Edmiston

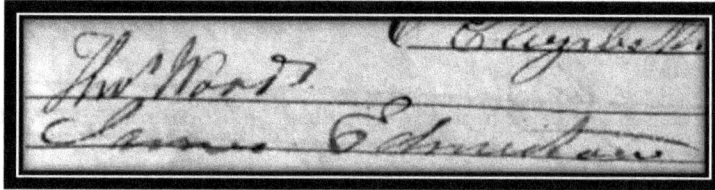

Signatures:

- Elizabeth Garrett & Richard Williams – 30 Jul 1637 (Marriage, **St. Michan Parish**)

- Elizabeth Garrett & William Kelly

  - Elizabeth Kelly – bapt. 14 Nov 1819 (Baptism, **SS. Michael & John Parish** (RC))

- Ellen Garrett & Cornelius (C o r n e l i u s) Driscoll

  - Mary Driscoll – bapt. 11 Feb 1836 (Baptism, **Aughadown Parish** (RC))

- Ellen Garrett & Daniel Bohane

  - James Bohane – bapt. Feb 1810 (Baptism, **Clontead Parish** (RC))

  - Mary Bohane – bapt. 25 Aug 1815 (Baptism, **Kinsale Parish** (RC))

- Ellen Garrett & Daniel Brohane – 9 Feb 1839 (Marriage, **Courcy's Country or Ballinspittal Parish** (RC))

  - John Brohane – bapt. 3 Jul 1845 (Baptism, **Courcy's Country or Ballinspittal Parish** (RC))

  - Daniel Brohane – bapt. 23 May 1857 (Baptism, **Courcy's Country or Ballinspittal Parish** (RC))

Wedding Witnesses:

Michael Ruby & Gerald Garrett

Garrett Surname Ireland: 1600s to 1900s

- Ellen Garrett & Daniel Murphy

  o Catherine Murphy – bapt. 14 May 1812 (Baptism, **Clontead Parish (RC)**)

- Ellen Garrett & Dennis Connolly – 11 Sep 1836 (Marriage, **Kinsale Parish (RC)**)

- Ellen Garrett & Dennis Murphy

  o Michael Murphy – bapt. Sep 1810 (Baptism, **Clontead Parish (RC)**)

- Ellen Garrett & Martin Ward

  o Charles Ward – b. 1859, bapt. 1859 (Baptism, **St. Andrew Parish (RC)**)

  o Ellen Ward – b. 11 Mar 1863, bapt. 13 Apr 1863 (Baptism, **SS. Michael & John Parish (RC)**)

  o Hannah Ward – b. 12 Dec 1866, bapt. 20 Dec 1866 (Baptism, **SS. Michael & John Parish (RC)**)

  o Frederick William Ward – b. 1870, bapt. 1870 (Baptism, **St. Andrew Parish (RC)**)

Martin Ward (father):

Residence - 41 King Street - 1859

4 Eustace Street - April 13, 1863

61 Upper Stephen's Street - December 20, 1866

40 Clarendon Street - 1870

- Ellen Garrett & Thomas Cummins

  o Jeremiah Cummins – bapt. 25 Jan 1817 (Baptism, **Kinsale Parish (RC)**)

  o Julie Cummins – bapt. 20 Sep 1819 (Baptism, **Kinsale Parish (RC)**)

- Ellen Garrett & Thomas Glennon – 17 Sep 1856 (Marriage, **Rathmines Parish (RC)**)

Hurst

- Frances Garrett & Bartholomew Cronin

  - Bartholomew Cronin – bapt. 16 Nov 1827 (Baptism, **Kinsale Parish (RC)**)

- Frances Rogan Garrett & Patrick Quinn

  - Peter Henry Quinn – bapt. 26 Feb 1837 (Baptism, **Rathmines Parish (RC)**)

  - Richard Quinn & Anne Allen – 26 Oct 1879 (Marriage, **Rathmines Parish (RC)**)

Richard Quinn (son):

Residence - Windsor Terrace - October 26, 1879

Anne Allen, daughter of Peter Allen & Mary Young (daughter-in-law):

Residence - Charlemont Street - October 26, 1879

- Frances Teresa Garrett & John Rogers – 22 May 1831 (Marriage, **Rathmines Parish (RC)**)

Wedding Witnesses:

Peter Garrett & Matthew Whelan

- Helen Garrett & Richard Lynch

  - James Roche – bapt. 10 Mar 1776 (Baptism, **Cork - SS. Peter & Paul Parish (RC)**)

- Honor Garrett & Cornelius (C o r n e l i u s) Caska – 11 Feb 1809 (Marriage, **Bantry Parish (RC)**)

Honor Garrett (wife):

Residence - Bantry - February 11, 1809

- Jane Garrett & John Donovan – 27 Sep 1842 (Baptism, **Courcy's Country or Ballinspittal Parish (RC)**)

Garrett Surname Ireland: 1600s to 1900s

Wedding Witnesses:

John Cahill & Ellen Garrett

- Jane Garrett & Terence Sullivan

    o Ellen Sullivan – bapt. 26 Jul 1839 (Baptism, **Clontead Parish** (RC))

- Joan Garrett & Bartholomew Daly – 15 Feb 1815 (Marriage, **Clontead Parish** (RC))

Wedding Witnesses:

Michael Garrett & John Daly

- Joan Garrett & John White

    o James White – b. 11 Feb 1810, bapt. 11 Feb 1810 (Baptism, **Killarney Parish** (RC))

John White (father):

Residence - Killarney - February 11, 1810

- Mabel Horatia Garrett & Charles Murphy

    o William Haughton Murphy – b. 9 Mar 1891, bapt. 9 Apr 1891 (Baptism, **St. Stephen Parish**)

Charles Murphy (father):

Residence - 15 Adelaide Road - April 9, 1891

Occupation - Barrister at Law - April 9, 1891

- Margaret Garrett & Dennis Murphy

    o Michael Murphy – bapt. Aug 1810 (Baptism, **Clontead Parish** (RC))

Hurst

- Margaret Garrett & Jeffery Dunby

  - James Dunby – bapt. 7 Jul 1831 (Baptism, **St. Nicholas Parish (RC)**)

- Margaret Garrett & John Horgan

  - John Horgan – bapt. 28 Jun 1816 (Baptism, **Kinsale Parish (RC)**)

- Margaret Garrett & John Magrath – 30 Nov 1845 (Marriage, **St. Mary, Pro Cathedral Parish (RC)**)

Wedding Witnesses:

John Page & Mary Page

- Margaret Garrett & John Wade – 2 Oct 1741 (Marriage, **St. Anne Parish**)

- Margaret Garrett & Joseph Plunkett – 24 Dec 1780 (Baptism, **St. Andrew Parish (RC)**)

Wedding Witnesses:

George McCann & Sarah Dowdall

- Margaret Garrett & Michael Hayes – 19 Jun 1843 (Marriage, **Kinsale Parish (RC)**)

- Margaret Garrett & Richard Maher

  - William Maher & Catherine O'Flanagan – 7 Jan 1884 (Marriage, **St. Mary, Pro Cathedral Parish (RC)**)

William Maher (son):

Residence - Thurles - January 7, 1884

Catherine O'Flanagan, daughter of Patrick O'Flanagan & Ellen O'Neill

(daughter-in-law):

Residence - Queens County - January 7, 1884

Garrett Surname Ireland: 1600s to 1900s

Wedding Witnesses:

Philip Ryan & Margaret O'Flanagan

- Margaret Garrett & Robert L'Estrange

  o Robert L'Estrange – b. 24 Feb 1878, bapt. 8 Mar 1878 (Baptism, **St. Nicholas Parish (RC)**)

Robert L'Estrange (father):

Residence - 5 Wood Street - March 8, 1878

- Mary Garrett & Branely John Branely

  o Bridget Branely – b. 17 Dec 1879, bapt. 12 Jan 1880 (Baptism, **SS. Michael & John Parish (RC)**)

Branely John Branely (father):

Residence - 7 Temple Bar - January 12, 1880

- Mary Garrett & Daniel Cronin – 5 Feb 1842 (Marriage, **Kinsale Parish (RC)**)

  o John Cronin – bapt. 14 Nov 1846 (Baptism, **Kinsale Parish (RC)**)

  o Catherine Cronin – bapt. 4 Mar 1853 (Baptism, **Kinsale Parish (RC)**)

Wedding Witnesses:

Dennis Cronin & Mick Murphy

- Mary Garrett & Edward Crofton

  o Anne Crofton – bapt. 11 Dec 1771 (Baptism, **St. Mary, Pro Cathedral Parish (RC)**)

- Mary Garrett & George Aery – 31 Jul 1655 (Marriage, **St. Michan Parish**)

- Mary Garrett & Gulielmo Hanling – 23 Jul 1845 (Marriage, **St. Michan Parish (RC)**)

Hurst

Wedding Witnesses:

Charles Brassington, Catherine Garrett, & Ellen Walsh

- Mary Garrett & James Quinlan

  - Thomas Quinlan – b. 1896, bapt. 1896 (Baptism, **St. Andrew Parish (RC)**)

James Quinlan (father):

Residence - 39 Poolbeg Street - 1896

- Mary Garrett & John Couch

  - Sarah Elizabeth Couch – b. 21 Mar 1880, bapt. 4 Apr 1880 (Baptism, **Rathmines Parish (RC)**)

John Couch (father):

Residence - Harold's Cross - April 4, 1880

- Mary Garrett & Robert Daly – 26 Jun 1806 (Marriage, **Dunleckney Parish**)

Mary Garrett (wife):

Residence - Dunleckney Parish - June 26, 1806

Robert Daly (husband):

Residence - Riledmond Parish - June 26, 1806

- Mary J. Garrett & James Gaynor

  - Mary Agnes Gaynor – b. 20 May 1873, bapt. 29 May 1873 (Baptism, **St. James Parish (RC)**)

Garrett Surname Ireland: 1600s to 1900s

James Gaynor (father):

Residence - Inchicore - May 29, 1873

- Mary Joan Garrett & John Kennedy

    o James Kennedy – b. 27 Oct 1882, bapt. 10 Nov 1882 (Baptism, **St. Agatha Parish (RC)**)

John Kennedy (father):

Residence - 11 Richmond Cottages - November 10, 1882

- Sarah Garrett & Thomas McGuirk – 6 Mar 1791 (Marriage, **St. Michan Parish (RC)**)

Wedding Witnesses:

Thomas Byrne & Elizabeth Connor

- Sarah Garrett & William Meredith – 20 Sep 1785 (Marriage, **St. Anne Parish**)

William Meredith (husband):

Occupation - Esquire - September 20, 1785

- Susan Garrett & Dane Hammond – Unclear (Marriage, **St. Werburgh Parish**)
- Susan Garrett & James O'Neill – 27 Feb 1797 (Marriage, **St. Michan Parish (RC)**)

Wedding Witnesses:

James Graydon & Bridget Graydon

Name Variations

Includes Latin and Abbreviated forms of names found in the original documents.

Abigail = Abigale, Abigall

Anne = Ann, Anna, Annae

Bartholomew = Barth, Bartholmeus, Bartholomeo

Bridget = Birgis, Brigid, Brigida, Bridgit

Catherine = Catharine, Catharina, Catharinae, Catherina, Cath, Catha, Cathae, Cathn, Kate

Charles = Carolus, Charls, Chas

Christopher = Christoph

Daniel = Danielem, Danielis

Edmund = Edmond

Edward = Ed, Edwd

Eleanor = Eleo, Eleonora, Elinor, Ellenor

Elizabeth = Betty, Elisa, Elisabeth, Eliz, Eliza, Elizab, Elizh, Elizth

Ellen = Elena, Ellena

Emily = Emilia

Esther = Essie, Ester

Francis = Fransicum

George = Geo, Georg, Georgius

Grace = Gratiae

Gulielmo = Guil, Guillelmi, Gulielmum, Guillelmus, Gulmi

Helen = Helena

Garrett Surname Ireland: 1600s to 1900s

Honor = Hanora, Honora

James = Jacobi, Jacobus, Jas

Jane = Joanna

Jeanne = Jeannae, Joannae

Joan = Johanna, Joney

John = Jno, Joannem, Joannes, Johannis

Joseph = Jos

Juliana = Julian

Leticia = Letitia, Lettice, Letticia

Lewis = Louis

Luke = Lucas

Margaret = Margarita, Margaritae, Margeret, Marget, Margt

Martha = Marthae

Mary = Maria, My

Mary Anne = Marianna, Marianne, Maryanne

Michael = Michaelis, Michl

Patrick = Pat, Patt, Patk, Patricii, Patricius

Peter = Petri

Richard = Ricardi, Ricardus, Rich, Richd

Robert = Roberti

Rose = Rosa, Rosae

Thomas = Thom, Thomae, Thoms, Thos, Ths

Timothy = Timotheus, Timy

William = Wil, Will, Willm, Wm

Notes

Notes

Notes

Notes

Notes

Notes

Index

A

B

Hurst

Bridget
- *1742 Mar 4* 60
- *1770 Nov 25* 53
- *1825 Feb 20* 44

Caroline Amelia
- *1889 Jul 21* 32

Catherine
- *1660 May 21* 36
- *1741 Apr 8* 34
- *1749 Dec 24* 59
- *1754 Oct 6* 34
- *1868 Oct 4* 23

Catherine Mary
- *1846* 59

Charles
- *1812 May 17* 73

Charlotte Amelia
- *1866 Aug 31* 84

Clare Henrietta Hall
- *1887 Jun 9* 25

Cornelius (C o r n e l i u s)
- *1809 May 30* 75

David
- *1823 Oct* 42
- *1860* 23

Edward
- *1697 Jan 3* 45

Edward Abraham
- *1876 Jan 2* 7

Edward Alexander Francis
- *1877 Dec 2* 10

Edward Christopher
- *1887 Mar 30* 12

Edward Garrett
- *1876 Sep 22* 80

Edward William
- *1864 Jul 20* 80

Eleanor
- *1862 Apr 20* 43, 69

Elizabeth
- *1692 Oct 2* 45
- *1740 Dec 17* 45
- *1746 Jun 3* 33
- *1746 Oct 13* 42
- *1759 Jun 28* 81
- *1767 Oct 10* 42
- *1795 May 3* 33
- *1857 Feb 15* 43
- *1862 Dec 21* 51
- *1874* 18

Elizabeth Jane Sarah
- *1890 Aug 10* 13

Elizabeth Lauder
- *1858 Feb 10* 60

Ellen
- *1811 Oct* 54
- *1822* 54
- *1828 Oct* 45
- *1838 Feb 28* 54
- *1855 Jul 4* 79

Ellen Mary
- *1843 Feb 8* 73
- *1892* 4

Emily Amelia
- *1894 Oct 14* 14

Evelyn Harriett
- *1874 Jul 2* 7

Florence Maude
- *1876 Jan 14* 85

Frances Emma
- *1858 Jan 1* 72

Francis
- *1834 Jul* 44

George
- *1810 May* 45
- *1823 Feb 23* 16
- *1858* 23

George Charles William
- *1882 Oct 8* 7

George Thomas
- *1852 Jun 27* 43

Georgina Caroline
- *1864 Aug 24* 84

Georgina Elizabeth
- *1887 Jan 30* 7

Gulielmo
- *1877 Apr 26* 5

Harriet Caroline

Hurst

Hurst

Garrett Surname Ireland: 1600s to 1900s

Garrett Surname Ireland: 1600s to 1900s

H

J

K

135

About The Author

Donovan Hurst graduated from San Diego State University with a Bachelor of Arts in the major field of studies of History and a minor in the field of studies of Anthropology. He is a current member of The General Society of Mayflower Descendants and has been conducting genealogical research for over 10 years tracing back his ancestors to their ancestral homelands in Denmark, England, France, Germany, Ireland, Norway, and Scotland.

www.ingramcontent.com/pod-product-compliance
Lightning Source LLC
Chambersburg PA
CBHW081416270326
41931CB00015B/3291